LONDON'S BEST PUBS

LONDON'S
BEST PUBS

Peter Haydon
with Tim Hampson

IMM lifestyle
books™
Read. Learn. Do What You Love.

Published 2016—IMM Lifestyle Books
www.IMMLifestyleBooks.com

IMM Lifestyle Books are distributed in the UK by Grantham Book Service,
Trent Road, Grantham, Lincolnshire, NG31 7XQ.

In North America, IMM Lifestyle Books are distributed by Fox Chapel Publishing,
1970 Broad Street, East Petersburg, PA 17520,
www.FoxChapelPublishing.com.

ISBN 978 1 5048 0020 4

10 9 8 7 6 5 4 3 2 1

Printed in China

CONTENTS

PREFACE TO THE 2016 EDITION

My father, who knows more about London than virtually anyone, says that currently it is enjoying a Golden Age. He maintains that he has never seen it more dynamic, vibrant, colourful and energetic; and he is 83. This dynamism is reflected in its pubs; hence the need for a new edition of this book.

Most of the pubs contained within these pages were in the first, second and third editions, for the simple reason that they are great, and almost timeless institutions in their own right. However, there has been quite a bit of churn. Some pubs have changed hands and lost their mojo. Some have stood still while others around them have gotten

better. Pubs take a lot of physical punishment and need frequent maintenance and occasional refurbishment. There is definite 'group think' in the contemporary pub refurbishment world, so some once interesting pubs have had a make-over that has rendered them bland and uniform. They are out. One or two have simply closed.

There are two distinct themes in the London pub scene that are reflected in some of the new entries in this book. The first is the rise of the craft beer scene, a very visible aspect of the current dynamism of London. When the last edition of this book was published there were 13 breweries in London. There are now more than 113 and the number continues to climb. I've spent more than 20 years of my life in the brewing industry, and I honestly have no idea what 'craft beer' is. That doesn't really matter, though, as with 'cool', if you have to ask it's not for you. However, whatever it is, it is a phenomenon that has had a huge impact on London's pubs. Mostly this is reflected in the fact that most pubs now offer a wider and more interesting range of beers, and interesting no longer just means real ale (I do know what that is). It is also reflected in the growing number of brewpubs in the capital. There are many more of these than we have space for, but we have been able to include a number of pioneering and trendsetting examples.

The other trend is the shift to the suburbs. Curiously, most of the pubs that have dropped out of these pages are located in central London. Most of the new entries are not. On one level this

is not surprising: young innovators can rarely afford the higher property premiums associated with established parts of town and often genuinely prefer the vibe of the less fashionable neighbourhoods (though there are ever fewer of these — London is enjoying a Golden Age, after all). It also means that a number of the new suburban pubs in this book may not have even been pubs in earlier lives. Imaginative thinking and reuse of old buildings is thus also an emerging trend in the London pub scene. The net effect of this move is that you will have to travel further to get around all the pubs in the book; for this I apologise. To Robert Louis Stephenson is attributed the modern take on an old Taoist proverb, to whit 'To journey hopefully is a better thing than to arrive'. I'm not sure I agree that the anticipation of the pint is better than the pint itself, but if you have to travel a little further to reach your goal, you will have deserved your pint all the more for it. I hope it tastes all the better for that.

PETER HAYDON

INTRODUCTION

There have been many attempts to try to understand why it is that the pub is such a peculiarly British thing. I owe my entire career to an attempt to answer this question, but I still do not think I truly know what the answer is. This book tries to offer some explanation of what a London pub is, as well as being a celebration of the best pubs in London. We have also tried to put the pub in the context of its surrounding streets, their inhabitants and trades, as a pub is shaped by its surroundings, by the flow of life past its doors, in the same way as water carves the contours of a river.

This book is also an historical document – a snap-shot of what London's best pubs looked like a decade into the 21st century. It is unlikely that the pubs shown will look exactly the same when you come to visit them. There will be subtle changes, repairs to the heavy wear and tear pubs suffer, subtle improvements, a change in atmosphere caused by a change in landlord, something intangible perhaps. It is also likely that at least one of the pubs will have been changed out of all recognition. All I can do, therefore, is present the pubs to you as they are today, lay out what we know about them as they were, and hope that tomorrow they retain their character and charm.

You might wonder what it was that qualified the 114 pubs in this volume for inclusion over the 5,500 other pubs in London. There was only one criterion used when assessing a pub's merit: I asked myself 'Would you thank me for recommending you to go here?', and I hope that you will.

When asking myself this question I had to have a yardstick against which to measure the pub. There needed to be some kind of test, and I chose what I call the Dr Johnson test. The 18th-century writer and critic's description of what made a tavern special for him is probably unsurpassable:

There is no private house in which people can enjoy themselves so well as at a capital tavern. Let there be ever so great a plenty of good things, ever so much grandeur, ever so much elegance, ever so much desire that everybody should be easy, in the nature of things it cannot be; there must always be some degree of care and anxiety. The master of the house is anxious to entertain his guests; the guests are anxious to be agreeable to him, and no man but a very impudent dog indeed can freely command what is another man's house as if it were a tavern, there is a general freedom from anxiety. You are sure you are welcome; and the more noise you make, the more trouble you give, the more good things you call for, the welcomer you are. No, Sir, there is nothing which has yet been contrived by man by which so much happiness is produced as by a good tavern or inn.

If, when you enter a pub, you feel uplifted and inclined to agree with Johnson that 'No, Sir', man's other contrivances are as mere fancy compared

'Work is the curse of the drinking class'.

Oscar Wilde

with a good inn, then the pub has passed the test.

Inevitably such a selection is fairly personal. Another author would certainly have included some other public houses and excluded some contained here. I have attempted to be broad in my selection, to ensure a fair geographic coverage as well as to offer something for everyone.

For me, the chief virtue of a pub is that it can be almost anything you want it to be. Provided you do the landlord the courtesy of buying a drink you can stay as long as you like, be as gregarious or as reticent as you like and be as idle or as studious as you like. You can enjoy the company of all or engage in a solitary reverie. You can talk to strangers, make lifelong friends, catch up on gossip, commit to memory a cracking good joke for later use, hold forth on any subject close to your heart and leave whenever you wish (within opening hours, of course). The pub is egalitarian, libertarian, non-judgmental and subversive. For these reasons alone, I rate it as priceless.

Naturally, there are different types of pub in different places. Country pubs are different from town pubs. Manchester pubs are different from Birmingham pubs and both are different from London pubs. Within London, East End pubs are different from west London pubs, and mews pubs differ from high-street pubs. At different periods London has grown at different rates and in different directions, and the pubs that have been thrown up as a result are shaped accordingly. Pubs also vary because they share a different lineage.

In the period from which our earliest surviving London pubs date, the 15th and 16th centuries, there were three types of 'pub' establishment – the alehouse, the tavern and the inn.

The Inn

The inn was defined by the provision of accommodation, and was separately licensed. It evolved from the custom of pilgrimage, and in Geoffrey Chaucer's The Canterbury Tales The Tabard Inn is a prime example. Naturally, the functions of inns grew as mobility increased, so that by the early 19th century the coaching inns were frequently grand affairs, important hot-houses of economic activity engaged in trade and the movement of goods, people and information. Today we have forgotten the high regard in which such institutions were held. The coaching era was a golden age for inns. People up and down the country would set their clocks and watches by the passage of the Royal Mail. The opium eater Thomas De Quincey (1785–1859) noted that coaches would start off from London and York at the same time and invariably meet at a bridge that marked the half-way point on the route.

The nation was hugely proud of its coaches and inns, and when they were killed off by the railways there was a genuine popular appreciation that something rather special had passed away. Only one London coaching inn survives today, The George Inn in Southwark.

'I have taken more out of alcohol than alcohol has taken out of me'.

Sir Winston Churchill

The Tavern

Taking their name from the Latin *tavernae*, taverns barely existed outside London and the ports until the 15th century. The tavern's heyday was undoubtedly the 18th century, and coincided with the emergence and rise of the new merchant classes who, in London at least, made the taverns and coffee houses peculiarly their own.

Although they sold ale, the drink of the taverns was wine. Before the introduction of gin into society in the late 17th century, wine was the only other widely available alcohol, but that was not for the masses. Wine held an ambiguous place in popular culture. Most people never touched it, and it could not be demonized as gin came to be because the Catholic Church had decreed, as early as the 6th century, that communion could only be celebrated with red wine made from grapes.

As a nation, we are presumed to have discovered wine only in the last 30 years or so, but we are poor consumers compared with our 18th-century forebears who downed very large quantities. However, since we were frequently at war with France, its legitimate supply was often uncertain. Our long-standing friendship with Portugal meant that port was the popular tavern drink of the 18th century. Consumed as it was in very large volumes, port can be considered largely responsible for having made the 18th century the era of gout and the skull-splitting hangover.

Taverns survive in a few examples, but were very much a victim of gin, since the effect of gin consumption was to make drunkenness no longer respectable. We tend to forget that for our 18th-century and earlier ancestors drunkenness across all classes was – among the English at least – a very frequent occurrence. Dr Johnson himself is supposed to have remarked on one occasion that, 'All decent people of Lichfield got drunk every night and were not the worse thought of.'

Ale and the Alehouse

Beyond coaching inns, another thing the nation was inordinately proud of was its ale. Ale was hugely important in the development of the country. I personally believe that ale is a necessary precondition for civilization. We know that ale – by which is meant a fermented grain drink – was available in the Tigris and Euphrates valley, the cradle of civilization, at a very early date. Some 1,500 years BC Egyptian students were neglecting their studies and spending too much time in the alehouses of the Nile. We also know that when western civilization expanded, the 'primitive' cultures that were discovered did not have ale.

Consumption of ale is also a distinction between nomadic and non-nomadic peoples, as production requires settlement, and settlement creates added problems of hygiene and pollution as people are spectacularly dirty. Ale was safe to drink because it was first boiled, and then made alcoholic. In this process any pathogens were killed and could not re-establish themselves. With the addition of hops in the early 15th century – when ale (unhopped) became beer (hopped) – the preservative qualities of this safe liquid were enhanced. Ale was a staple, therefore, at a time when any settlement was likely to pollute springs and wells.

Ale was not only a staple drink but an important means of payment underpinning the feudal economy. The alehouse was an essential feature of any community, and increased in importance as feudal hierarchies broke down after the Black Death and as brewing in the manor house declined. Ale and the alehouse permitted the growth of communities and with them economic development. Subsequently, a general awareness of ale's importance manifested itself in a national pride in the quality and strength of ale and beer, and this pride was shared across all classes of society until the mid-18th century. This common feeling survived the best efforts of the Puritans to suppress alehouses and the general enjoyment of anything 'profane' in the 17th century, and started to evaporate only with the introduction and popularity of gin.

Under the Influence of Gin

The pub as we know it today is a direct descendant of the rude alehouse, shaped by exposure to gin. As part of his anti-French policies, William III (1650–1702) popularized gin in order to reduce the popularity of wine, but succeeded only in making the nation drunk. So, with gin came the revelation that there was an alcoholic drink that was actually bad

for people. The impact of this on the 18th-century mind, conditioned as it was by hundreds of years of faith in the virtues of ale, we cannot start to comprehend, and all pubs everywhere have been affected by this profound truth.

The 1740s were the worst years of the first gin fever. It was immortalized by William Hogarth in his famous prints *Gin Lane* and *Beer Street*, in which he contrasted the effects of the foul, poisonous, adulterated gin that stupefied people and rendered them incapable of work with the hearty jollity that came from honest and nutritious beer. Hogarth was making a point to a populace who understood his message painfully well. Between 1749 and 1751

the population of London was estimated to have fallen by over 9,300 as a result of gin consumption, confirming the prescience of those fears expressed around the turn of the century: 'Tis a growing vice among the common people and may in time prevail as much as Opium with the Turks, to which many attribute the scarcity of people in the East.'

The fall in population was also a result of a high death rate accompanying a low birth rate. At the time there were no major outbreaks of disease, London's population density was falling and people's diet was improving as corn prices were low and there were few bad harvests. Meat was fairly cheap and there was a rapid expansion in the market garden industry. There were also improvements in the sanitary facilities in the metropolis. All these factors should have conspired to produce a population explosion, and the fact that the population did not increase, but actually fell, was blamed unequivocally on gin.

Tamed By Temperance

By causing such massive trauma to the nation's health and wealth, gin paved the way for the Temperance movement and anti-drink lobbies of the 19th century.

The effect of the first gin fever was to detach the middle and upper classes from the universal enjoyment of drink and to create an increasing intolerance of over-indulgence. By the time the second gin fever broke out in the 1830s, sufficient time had elapsed (not to mention other social transformations such as the Industrial Revolution with all that that meant for social values, living conditions and class differences) for the response to be much more earnest and organized.

The Temperance movement of the 19th century was a massive political campaign. By the late 19th century and early 20th drink was a political issue. W. E. Gladstone, leader of the Liberal Party, was famously 'borne down in a torrent of gin and beer' in the 1874 election. The Liberal and Tory parties were split on pro-Temperance and pro-trade lines. Opposition to

Tom and Jerry "Masquerading it" among the Cadgers in the "Back Slums", in the Holy Land.

Drawn & Eng.^d by I.R. & G. Cruickshank.

the draconian and hugely unjust 1908 licensing bill, which had an affect on the activity, appearance and number of pubs, provoked demonstrations in Hyde Park that attracted 800,000 people.

One effect of the bill was to bar individuals with brewing connections from sitting on magistrates' licensing benches, while individuals with Temperance sympathies actively insinuated themselves onto benches. Justices of the Peace, who ever since 1255 had been tasked with regulating the supply of drink to ensure that there was an adequate supply of ale for the nation, started flagrantly to abuse this power by trying to restrict the availability of alcohol. Benches acted outrageously, making capricious decisions, often *ultra vires* and usually without regard for the loss of livelihood of the publican and his family. Not for nothing was the activity of the benches called a 'tyranny'.

The effect of this was to make licences increasingly rare. Those places whose licences were not suppressed had to be made respectable in order to avoid suppression. At the same time, in the 1880s, the first of the brewery flotations took place – starting with Guinness. Its 1886 flotation was over-subscribed some 50 times and raised a staggering £6 million. Brewing companies rushed to float. They merged and bought each other up in order to become better flotation prospects, and numerous successful flotations meant that the trade was awash with money.

The London Pub

In London there had been a gentlemanly system whereby brewers did not tend to own pubs, but secured their access to the market by the vastly cheaper ploy of 'tying' publicans to them by way of loans. Outside London, breweries increasingly

owned their pubs, a practice that had come about as a reaction to endemic adulteration at the start of the 19th century. The newly cash-rich brewers, and those from outside London in particular, started buying London pubs. On the defensive, the London brewers started buying them too. The result was an orgy of spending that varied in nature according to the government of the day.

When the Liberals were in power the tendency was to refurbish public houses to attract custom in an increasingly competitive market and improve the house in order that magistrates would be more likely to suppress another. Under Tory administrations licences were felt to be more secure and larger numbers of pubs would be bought by brewers and more public houses would be commissioned from architects and builders. The two-party system, therefore, was very effective at completely changing the appearance of public houses. Expansion under Tories would

be followed by retrenchment under Liberals, which would lead to increased pressure to buy under Tories. The whole together created a highly inflationary spiral.

The Crown in Cricklewood Broadway, for example, was sold in 1873 for £2,000. It was sold again for £5,000, then £15,000, £32,000, £42,000 and in 1898 it achieved £86,000. The upward spiral was a speculator's bonanza, and the entry of non-trade interests fuelled inflation. The Cannon Brewery of Clerkenwell spent £1,363,010 on acquiring 125 pubs between 1893 and 1898, paying maximum amounts in each year of £23,000, £24,500, £28,200, £50,000, £55,000 and £86,000, in addition to the £250,000 spent on rebuilding or refurbishing their new acquisitions.

Once acquired, pubs had to recoup the inflated prices that had been paid for them. In order to do this they had to attract more custom, and to attract more custom the pub had to be rebuilt or refurbished. Frequently, pubs that had been redecorated in the late 1880s would be further redecorated or rebuilt in the 1890s. The net effect of all this was to ensure that very few surviving town pubs date back much earlier than the 1880s. The other effect was to make the speculation and Temperance-driven spiral unsustainable. In the late 1890s an increasing number of bankruptcies among publicans and brewers who had spent more on their pubs than they could ever hope to recover led to an almighty property crash.

Beer Today, Gone Tomorrow

The consequences of this crash were two-fold. Firstly, it meant that there was very little pub building after around 1898, so while London pubs may date from any of the last six centuries, their surviving fabric is likely to date from a relatively short period – the 1880s and 1890s.

The second is that the bankruptcies led to a further concentration of pub ownership. For most of the 20th century, London was characterized by a very small number of free houses competing with ever larger combines of brewers offering an ever smaller selection of beers.

This came to a head in 1989 when the Monopolies and Mergers Commission produced its report, 'The Supply of Beer', which concluded that the big brewery combines were effectively running a monopoly that operated against the public interest.

The history of the British brewing industry since that fateful report has been a sorry one, in large part because the politicians made a hash of implementing the report's recommendations. The result is that today, instead of most pubs being owned by brewers, most are owned by pub companies that are little more than property management firms.

The old brewery firms were in the business of selling beer and in order to do that they needed pubs. They therefore had a vested interest in ensuring that the pub fulfilled its traditional functions in the community, and consequently were fairly philanthropic, as indeed are those brewery firms that still do own pub estates – in London they are principally Fuller's, though others like Shepherd

Neame (Kent), Hall and Woodhouse (Dorset), McMullens (Hertfordshire), Adnams (Suffolk), Harveys (East Sussex) and Sam Smith's (Yorkshire) also have small toe-holds in the London market. Today's pub companies do not need to sell beer; they need only one thing – a guaranteed income stream to service their debt obligations. This means that if a pub can generate more cash in the short term by being sold off as a private house then they will sell it.

This is a particular problem in the countryside where it is estimated that six pubs a week are closing and that 50 per cent of Britain's rural population has no easy access to a local pub.

In the town this means that if a pub can generate more revenue as a car park, then it will become a car park. It also leads to the creation of superpubs. If there are only so many pounds in people's pockets earmarked for spending in the pub then it makes little sense to run 10 pubs in any community when encouraging them all to go to just one or two pubs is so much more profitable. This means that pub company investment is channelled away from 'community' pubs towards larger 'town centre' venues. It then becomes usual for the community pubs to be sold or closed because they have become unviable.

The effect of all this has been to create a highly undesirable state of affairs. The pub, far from being a centre of the community, where common and local identities are forged, where civic values are instilled, where much local philanthropy takes place and, most importantly, where people still have the increasingly rare chance to engage with people of other generations, is increasingly becoming homogenized. High streets increasingly resemble each other, lined with identikit branded pubs aimed at a narrow market segment and offering an equally narrow, cost effective range of core products.

The social consequences of this shift in pub culture during the 1990s caused very little popular debate until recently. However, with the Licensing Act 2003, which came into effect in 2005, Britain's arcane licensing laws were at last revised. The new law replaced over 50 existing laws regulating the licensing of premises and one of the key objectives was to facilitate flexible opening hours. Licences are now under local authority control and although they require the views of residents, businesses and the local authority to be taken into consideration before being granted, they are technically more accommodating.

The Future

Pubs are the most dynamic and versatile elements of the built environment. They also suffer a degree of sustained battery and are always being repaired or remodelled. In addition, the smoking ban which took effect in July 2007 has resulted in the refurbishment, for the most part sympathetic, of many of London's best pubs, allowing them to cater to a changing clientèle and making them generally more pleasant places to visit.

It is likely that by the time you visit the pubs listed here that there may well be changes from the scenes described and illustrated. Pubs do not stand still. Nor do breweries. The brewing landscape of London has suffered considerable trauma over the last five years. The Guinness brewery in Park Royal, North London, closed in 2005, shut by owners Diageo. Synonymous with Wandsworth, Youngs was part of the furniture of London until September 2006. Its pubs live on as operating outlets of yet another property company and the beers are brewed in Bedford. It remains to be seen whether, like Siamese twins separated by surgery, the Youngs beer brands and the pubs can survive without intimate connection with the missing twin. Certainly the romance associated with this previously much loved institution has evaporated. Happily there are other brewery companies willing to step into

the breach, just as there are plenty of idealistic and imaginative operators providing the great beer, food and service that the corporately owned pubs cannot.

If you love great pubs, as I do, then you must visit them and show the people in them that you care about what they do. They will repay you a thousand fold. I hope this book will take you into pubs that you might not otherwise have visited and that they will give you great pleasure once you are there. This is, after all, why they are there.

PETER HAYDON

Where to go if you like...

Real ales

Many of the pubs in this book are notable for their excellent choice of real ales and the list that follows is not exhaustive.

Euston Tap, p.40
The Harp, p.46
Fox & Anchor, p.73
The Jerusalem Tavern, p.78
Ye Olde Mitre Tavern, p.96
The Bohemia, p.126
Brewhouse and Kitchen, p.127
The Craft Beer Co., p.130
The Jolly Butchers, p.136
The Junction Tavern, p.138
Southampton Arms, p.146
The Wenlock Arms, p.150
The White Horse, p.189
The Beer Shop London, p.196
The Dog and Bell, p.198
The Market Porter, p.207
The Rake, p.210

Belgian beers

The Bohemia, p.126
The Cow, p.161
The White Horse, p.189
The Dog and Bell, p.198
The Rake, p.210

Unusual breweries

Euston Tap, p.40
  (Thornbridge Brewery)
The Porterhouse, p.52
  (Porterhouse Brewery)
The Jerusalem Tavern, p.78
  (St Peter's Brewery)
The Bohemia, p.126
Brewhouse and Kitchen, p.127
The Craft Beer Co., p.130
The Jolly Butchers, p.136
  (BrewDog)
The Greenwich Union, p.203
  (Meantime Brewing Company)
The Rake, p.210

THE WEST END

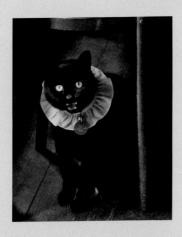

Soho, Covent Garden, Leicester Square and Piccadilly are all places synonymous with eating, drinking and entertainment, and have been for centuries. The drinking holes of Soho have long been frequented by both die-hard beer and whisky drinkers, such as Jeffrey Bernard, Dylan Thomas and Francis Bacon, and the more refined celebrities who love to quaff champagne at the surprisingly unpretentious French House. Around Covent Garden and Piccadilly the pubs attract the pre- and post-theatre crowds, while those pubs on the roads off frenetic Oxford Street may well be visited by the more adventurous tourist with a thirst who is seeking not only a drink but also some peace, quiet and tradition.

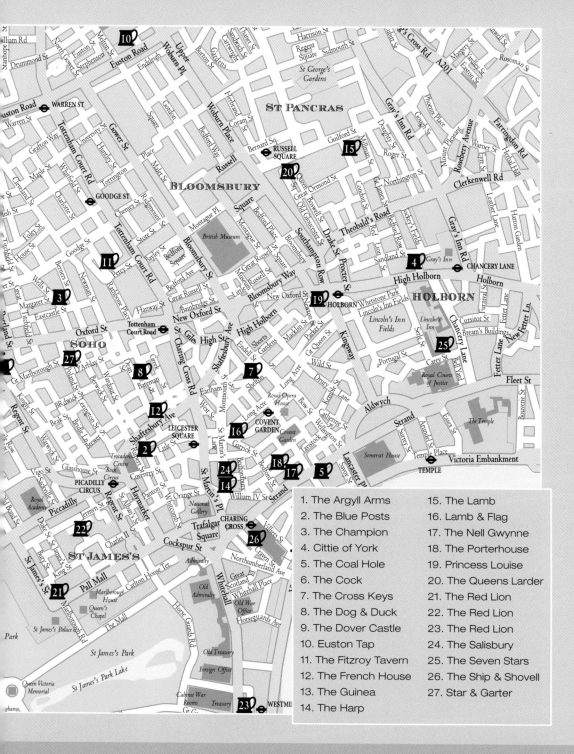

1. The Argyll Arms
2. The Blue Posts
3. The Champion
4. Cittie of York
5. The Coal Hole
6. The Cock
7. The Cross Keys
8. The Dog & Duck
9. The Dover Castle
10. Euston Tap
11. The Fitzroy Tavern
12. The French House
13. The Guinea
14. The Harp
15. The Lamb
16. Lamb & Flag
17. The Nell Gwynne
18. The Porterhouse
19. Princess Louise
20. The Queens Larder
21. The Red Lion
22. The Red Lion
23. The Red Lion
24. The Salisbury
25. The Seven Stars
26. The Ship & Shovell
27. Star & Garter

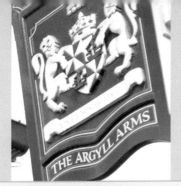

The Argyll Arms

18 Argyll Street, Soho W1F 7TP

BEERS: Truman's Runner, Fuller's London Pride, Reverend James, plus 6 guests

Busy pub just behind Oxford Circus; it has retained its original 1860s interior including etched glass and an ornate plaster ceiling

Given its location, it is to be expected that The Argyll has to treat with the tourist trade on a large scale, and given the splendour of The Argyll, passing tourists would be missing out if they did not pop in. The pub takes its name from the Duke of Argyll, one of Marlborough's generals, whose London mansion stood on the site now occupied by the nearby London Palladium. Both this pub and an earlier Argyll Arms dating from 1716 were torn down in the 1860s. The present building dates from 1866, but, unlike many of its contemporaries, it was not remodelled or expanded in the 1880s or 1890s and retains much of its original interior. In fact, one could go so far as to say that it is the best-kept pub of its kind anywhere.

Fine etched and engraved glass splits the pub into a number of booths, affording privacy from strangers in neighbouring booths. To the rear an open dining area offers an excellent view of the magnificently ornate plaster ceiling, as well as an unusual profile of your own head, since it also contains a large number of mirrors.

Voluptuously dark in colour, with a rich mahogany bar running the entire length of the pub, this is a fairly close approximation of what the Victorian pub was like. If you can exercise your imagination, suspend belief and block out the piped music you might just conjure up a similar scene, smokier and smellier, perhaps, with all kinds of Victorian street characters passing to and fro – bowler-hatted Hackney drivers, flat-capped costermongers, top-hatted gentlemen, all busily engaged in the hectic task of relaxation.

The Blue Posts

28 Rupert Street, Soho W1D 6DJ

BEERS: Timothy Taylor Landlord, Fuller's London Pride, Black Sheep Bitter

Intimate, wood-floored pub with a good range of cask beers complemented by good choices from Belgium

For many years, Piccadilly Circus – at the junction of five busy streets – has been a London Landmark. At its heart is a 19th-century bronze fountain topped by the figure of a winged archer; although it is commonly referred to as Eros, the pagan god of love, it was in fact intended to represent Anteros, the god of unrequited love and a symbol of Christian charity, as a monument to Lord Shaftesbury, a philanthropist.

Built in 1819 to connect Regent Street with the major shopping street of Piccadilly, the circus gives onto Shaftesbury Avenue as well as the Haymarket, Coventry Street and Glasshouse Street. Its closeness to major shopping and entertainment areas and its central location at the heart of the West End, have made Piccadilly Circus a busy meeting place.

A nearby pub, however, is an even better place to meet friends: the Blue Posts is a small, friendly bar, just a few moments' walk from the pulsations of Piccadilly Circus. A corner pub, it stands on Rupert Street and Rupert Close, with part of the pub forming an archway entrance into the close. It is a good place to meet for a drink or two, but ensure you are clear which Blue Posts pub you will be in – the name is shared with a pub on Berwick Street, the other side of Shaftsbury Avenue.

A pub is believed to have stood on this site since at least 1739. The name comes from the fact that the pillars outside were originally painted blue as an easy means of identification before a numbering system for buildings was introduced in the 18th century. 'Blue Posts' was simply used as a description of the place concerned and not its name as such – this Blue Posts no longer has pillars outside but at least the exterior is painted blue.

This is very much a locals pub, but no less friendly because of it. The busy, intimate, wood-floored pub is dominated by a large open bar behind which sits a watchful collection of China cats. Drinkers either sit at one of the six small tables, perch on a stool by the bar or simply stand.

To one side of the bar is a smaller space, which serves as a snug, in addition to another bar area upstairs where weekly quiz nights are held. The ground and first floors of the pub have been tastefully modernized with neo-Georgian woodwork.

In addition to its range of cask beers there is a good collection of bottled beers including some good choices from Belgium. There is also live jazz on Sunday every week.

The Champion

13 Wells Street, Fitzrovia W1T 3PA

BEERS: Sam Smith's Old Brewery Bitter, Sam Smith's Pure Brewed Organic Lager

Fantastic Sam Smith's pub with Victorian-style stained glass fit to outclass many an English country church

There is no more appropriate name for this pub, which is just one huge celebration of excellence. However, beware, as all is not what it seems – very little in this 'Victorian' boozer actually predates 1953.

The pub was originally named after Tom Figgs, an 18th-century prize-fighter who was the first to be recognized as a 'champion', and the building stands on the site of a booth where Figgs made a living teaching boxing. The pub fell into disrepair in the post-war years – as did many – and it was

refurbished in the 1950s in the Victorian style, with Toby jugs on the walls and a collection of Victorian china spirit and wine barrels overhead.

The pub, however, was once more allowed to run down over the years, until it was rescued in 1989 by the Yorkshire brewery firm of Sam Smith's. The brewery really went to town on the pub, installing stained-glass windows by Yorkshire artist Anne Sotheran to outclass those of many an English country church. The windows celebrate the best of British in a range of endeavours, and individuals commemorated include, among others, the explorer David Livingstone; the first cross-Channel swimmer Captain Matthew Webb, who died trying to swim the Niagara Falls; Edward Whymper, conqueror of the Matterhorn; the Earl of Mayo, Viceroy of India; the cricketer W. G. Grace; Florence Nightingale, Crimean war nurse; and Bob Fitzsimon, champion boxer. All in all an eclectic bunch, though champions all. Meanwhile, champion heavy-horse stallions are commemorated on the stairs, and pioneers in the worlds of science and engineering are remembered in the upstairs bar and dining room.

The Champion is a hugely successful pub, not least for being a very expensive practical joke in that the majority of its customers will believe that it is an authentic Victorian or Edwardian pub. There is a clue, however: Captain Bertie Dwyer, erstwhile president of the St Moritz tobogganing club and hero of the Cresta Run, died only in 1967, and this is recorded in the 'Victorian' stained glass.

Cittie of York

22 High Holborn, Holborn WC1V 6BS

BEERS: Sam Smith's Old Brewery Bitter

With its baronial hall-cum-cloister interior, the Cittie of York must rank as one of London's most eccentric public houses.

If you have visited the Princess Louise (see pp.54–55) on High Holborn and viewed its Victorian opulence, then another 'must visit' destination is Ye Olde Mitre Tavern (see pp.96–97) at the other end of Holborn. En route drop into the Cittie of York for a taste of the bogus and the bizarre.

This pub is an early example of the reaction to the gin palace architectural style that was to develop into the mediocre Brewers' Tudor of the 1920s and 1930s. In the inter-war years the brewing industry was so desperate to gentrify pubs in order to 'out-Temperance' the Temperance movement that it decided that a pub could resemble anything that wasn't a pub. This establishment's 'Merrie England' overtones were clearly an inspiration for much of what followed.

The amazing thing about the Cittie of York is that it resembles nothing and everything. The frontage is reminiscent of the great medieval coaching inns, such as the Angel at Grantham or the George at Glastonbury, while the long main bar cannot seemingly decide whether it is a porter tun room, a baronial hall or a real tennis court. Tudor bay windows sit over Art Nouveau arches. The booths along the east wall are a cross between church confessionals and Great Western Railway train compartments, and throughout all runs a mysterious 'HR' motif.

The most striking features of the long bar are the wine *tonneaux* ('casks'), which allegedly saw service until the start of the Blitz when they were drained and never refilled. Their presence is ironic as butts and casks of similar size were very much a feature of original 1820s and 1830s gin palaces – the precursors of the later Victorian style that the Cittie of York was a reaction against. Sadly, no original gin palace casks of this size survive anywhere.

There has been an inn on this site since 1430, but it has only been known under its present name since 1979, when it was acquired by the Yorkshire brewery Sam Smith's, which has done more to preserve London's pub history and heritage than any London brewery. If the long bar is not to your taste then try the small wood-panelled front bar or, if you are eating, the cellar bar, both in very different styles again.

The Coal Hole

91 Strand WC2R 0DW

BEERS: Nicholson's Pale Ale, Truman's Runner, Sharp's Doom Bar, Fuller's London Pride, plus guests

The Coal Hole's interior is a hotchpotch of styles and themes, creating something of an enigma

This unusual pub occupies a frontage of the Savoy Hotel building and is full of mysteries. What is the meaning of the SWL motif repeated in its leaded windows? Who are the maidens represented picking grapes on the frieze round the walls? What are the three strange objects in stained glass over the side entrance – cabbages or hearts? What is the significance of the three painted coats of arms bearing the names Beaufort, Savoy and John O'Gaunt? Why is the pub called The Coal Hole? Sadly, no answers are to be found in the pub. One can learn, however, that the actor Edmund Kean founded the Wolves Club for fellow actors here in 1815; and no doubt he retired here after his theatrical exertions at the nearby Lyceum, which he helped make famous.

The present fabric dates only from 1904, hence the slightly Art Nouveau feel to the place, which sits oddly with the equally slight medieval tone created by the leaded windows, stone and dark beams.

The date is surprising in itself, since during the 1880s and 1890s there was a massive pub price explosion which inevitably led to a crash, with the result that around 1904 very few pubs were being built (a notable exception being The Black Friar (see pp.68–69). Its date can be explained by the fact that it was part of the large Savoy development. Indeed, the motif in the windows may stand for Savoy Wine Lodge, though the owner believes that it could mean Strand Wine Lodge.

The pub takes its name from an early 18th-century landlord known as the singing collier, who would encourage customers, including cartoonists Gillray and Rowlandson, to join in with the musical entertainment. The original pub was demolished in the 1880s to make way for the Savoy Hotel, but when the wine lodge was opened in almost the same location Londoners typically continued to refer to it by its old name, so The Coal Hole it remained.

The Cock

27 Great Portland Street, Marylebone W1W 8QG

BEERS: Sam Smith's Old Brewery Bitter

A handsome Victorian pub with many period features, including its original, opulent snob screens

Great Portland Street is at the heart of London's rag trade, which extends off it along Margaret Street and Great Castle Street. The Cock, being well situated towards the Oxford Street end of the thoroughfare that bisects the Portland estate, is a great place to pick up some local history. James Boswell – Samuel Johnson's acolyte and inventor of the modern biography – died in a building on the site of what is now 122 Great Portland Street in 1795, and other famous local residents included the composer Carl Maria von Weber, the libertarian Leigh Hunt and the painter David Wilkie; meanwhile Pagani's – one of London's earliest restaurants – was on the site of number 42.

Oxford Street runs along an old Roman road, and takes its name not because it was known in the 1680s as the 'road to Oxford', but because in 1713 the north side of the road had been acquired by the Second Earl of Oxford, whose daughter married the Duke of Portland; their family connections provided the inspiration for many of the street names in the area. Oxford Street's history could occupy a book in itself. It was the haunt of Thomas De Quincey, the opium eater; while every day the ruined Harry Gordon Selfridge made a sad figure standing in front of his own store – from which he was banned to stop his lavish ways from bankrupting it.

Both these characters would have known of The Cock, and today it is still a handsome Victorian pub with many original features. In particular, the pub's snob screens are still in their original locations. The idea behind the snob screen – a small frosted-glass window at head height that could be swivelled open – was that it allowed you to order drinks from the bar staff without your face being visible to customers in other booths or bars. This was of particular concern to the highly class-conscious Victorians, especially those in trade, who would not want their social inferiors or junior colleagues seeing what, when or how much they were drinking. This was especially important during this period as work and home were much more closely intertwined: you could not escape back to the suburbs to gain anonymity as you were much more likely to live in the neighbourhood where you worked. In addition, London business life was much more street-focused. In The Cock, however, we can be grateful that the Victorian desire for privacy from prying eyes and gossip created such opulence.

The Cross Keys

31 Endell Street, Covent Garden WC2H 9BA

BEERS: Redemption Pale Ale, Truman's Runner

Permanently illuminated by a diffuse copper glow and festooned with an eclectic range of bric-a-brac, as many Victorian pubs once were

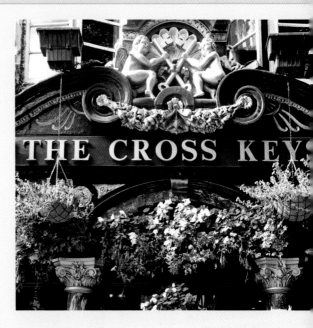

In 1101 Queen Matilda founded a leper hospital and dedicated it to St Giles, the patron saint of outcasts. Her prescience was astonishing: St Giles was the parish in which the Great Plague of 1665 started; in the 18th and 19th centuries it was notorious as the poorest parish in London and home to Irish immigrants. In the 19th century the spire of Henry Flitcroft's St Giles-in-the-Fields church was one of the most recognizable and most notorious features of the London skyline. Well into the 19th century the population of this small and self-contained neighbourhood was known to have a life expectancy well below the rest of the metropolis. It was in Endell Street (named after a rector of St Giles), in the shadow of St Giles-in-the-Fields church, that The Cross Keys was built in 1848.

The creation of Endell Street was a much-needed slum-clearance measure. It must have been in the spirit of hope that The Cross Keys – the symbol of St Peter, key holder to the gates of heaven – was named. It was probably in the spirit of protection too, since not even the slum clearances to the north could disguise the fact that Covent Garden to the south was also an area of brothels and whores, who may have used The Cross Keys as a place to pick up customers or stop for refreshment.

Today's pub is a glorious fusion of modern London and Londoners' taste for Victoriana. As far as Victorian clutter goes The Cross Keys is a prize winner, full of authentic bric-à-brac: antique clocks that still tell the time, a cricket bat signed by the legendary Don Bradman, enough copper hanging from the ceiling to make customers wary during a thunderstorm, all interwoven with a newer generation of bric-à-brac – Beatles memorabilia to be precise.

The whole pub is lit by a diffused light that has the feel of gas and cleverly brings out the richer tones and shades of an old London pub. Bright it is not, but hopefully this will not detract from your perusal of the countless treasures housed here. Beers from Brodie's Brewery, Leyton, dominate the bar.

The Dog & Duck

18 Bateman Street, Soho W1D 3AJ

BEERS: Nicholson's Pale Ale, Truman's Runner, plus 6 or 7 guest ales

One of London's best examples of the use of tiled panels, featuring bespoke dog and duck designs

The Dog & Duck is one of a number of Soho pubs whose names refer to the days when the area was a royal hunting ground. Today, this busy street corner pub is used by many media people on the hunt for a great idea that will bring them fame.

The Dog & Duck's long history has enabled numerous famous people to pass through its door. There has been a pub of this name in this part of Soho since 1743, which means Wolfgang Amadeus Mozart may well have been familiar with it when he lodged with his father and sister at No. 20 Frith Street between 1764 and 1765 (although it is doubtful he was ever a customer, having been only nine years old at the time). In March 1765 Mozart senior placed

an announcement in *The Public Advertiser* to the effect that 'Those Ladies and Gentlemen, who will honour him with their company... may... hear this young music master... perform in private, by giving him any thing to play at sight...' Thus it is likely that regulars of The Dog & Duck would have been aware of the young prodigy.

Other illustrious personages who may have patronized the pub include painters John Constable and Dante Gabriel Rossetti. George Orwell is known to have used the pub, and another famous likely customer was John Logie Baird, who used his bedroom at No. 22 Frith Street to give the first public demonstration of television to members of the Royal Institution on 26 January 1926. The apparatus Baird used in the demonstration is now on display in the Science Museum.

The present pub dates from 1897, and contains a large quantity of the highly glazed tiles that were a popular pub decoration of the time. Indeed, it is one of London's best examples of the use of tiled panels: at the back of the pub they resemble hung tapestries and at the front they extend down to the floor incorporating bespoke dog and duck designs. The architect, Francis Chambers, was careful to enclose the exterior in glazed tiles too, above the height of the grey marble on the ground floor. Take a moment to glance up and see the dog and duck high up on the pub wall. The front part of the pub is a narrow space between the bar and the particularly fine Victorian mirrors on the party wall. The bar's unusual location against the wall rather than against the windows is delightfully eccentric.

The Dover Castle

43 Weymouth Mews, Westminster W1G 7EH

BEERS: Sam Smith's Old Brewery Bitter, Sam Smith's Pure Brewed Organic Lager, Sam Smith's Taddy Lager

The place to visit after a walk in nearby Regent's Park; its discreet location is due to its 18th-century origins

Nearby Portland Place was the grandest street in London in the 18th century. Laid out by Robert and James Adam around 1778, its exceptional width was the result of an order given by Lord Foley that the view northwards from the windows of his house – now the Langham Hotel – should not be obscured.

The street has an illustrious history. It is home to the headquarters of the BBC, several embassies, the Medical Research Council and the Royal Institute of British Architects. Lord Byron courted Anne Isabella Milbanke at No. 63, author John Buchan lived at No. 76 between 1912 and 1919, and from 1863 to 1866 No. 98 was the American Embassy; historian Henry Brooks Adams lived at the embassy while working for his father Charles Adams, Abraham Lincoln's ambassador to the Court of St James.

Considering this heritage, it is no surprise to learn that there are no pubs on Portland Place. So, if you have just been to a radio recording at Broadcasting House or enjoyed a stroll in Regent's Park and need refreshment, The Dover Castle is the place to go. Named after the Roman castle above the port of Dover, it dates back to around 1750 and has been licensed since 1777. Its discrete location behind the grand houses accounts for a less lavish interior compared with its near neighbour The Cock (see p.36).

The fact that the well-to-do did not want pubs as neighbours did not mean that they did not need their services. This is demonstrated on the front of The Dover Castle where, instead of the normal descriptions of 'public' and 'saloon', the doors are inscribed 'retail' and 'bottle', indicating that at one door the customers could come in and sit down for refreshment as usual, while at the other they would be served beers and wines to be taken away to supply the needs of the great houses. Today it is a luncheon pub popular with BBC staff, architects and doctors from the surrounding institutions, who can enjoy a reasonably priced meal in a variety of settings, given the various snugs and rooms.

Famous clientele include musicians such as The Who, who used it as a watering hole between sessions at the recording studios that stand opposite the pub.

Euston Tap

Euston Station, West Lodge, 190 Euston Road NW1 2EF

BEERS: An exotic range of rare draft and bottled beers from the four corners of the earth.

A former railway parcels office which is now a temple to the diversity of beer culture

Pubs bring old buildings back to life. The Euston Tap, which opened in 2010 has given vibrancy and vitality to a disused railway parcels office which stands as one of two gate houses at the entrance to the 1960s façade that is now Euston station.

Built in 1837 the Grade II listed building is the last vestige of the once imposing Doric arch entrance to the original station. The archway was built as a grandiose portal to the brave new world of travel which the railways bought. But the Portland stone structure was demolished in 1961, with the rubble being dropped into the River Lea in East London to fill a hole in the Prescott Channel.

Today the Euston Tap is an entrance to craft beers from across the world. Two large imposing doors lead to the small downstairs bar, which is dominated by a large American-style back bar and its array of beer taps. Either side stand two tall fridges filled with bottled beers. To one side a spiral staircase leads up to a private section.

But it is downstairs where the action is – it might be small but it has a big atmosphere. On one wall hangs a copy of the Meilgaard beer flavour wheel, which helps drinkers identify the different tastes and smells a beer can have. And what a choice of flavoursome beers there are – eight cask and 19 kegs – with a range of beers from the UK, America, Belgium, Germany and even further afield. And if this is not enough there are more than 100 different bottled beers. With altbiers, kolsh, kellerbier, fruit beer, Black American IPAs and pumpkin beers there is something for everyone.

The Tap's cellar, which is housed underground in a former rifle range, is accessible only via a manhole cover. The space is so small and narrow that much of the equipment had to be taken apart and then reassembled once inside. But it is the rare beers which are in most people's sights, including several from the innovative Thornbridge brewery in Derbyshire, the impressive hop happy Port Brewing from America and several Czech masterpieces including an unfiltered Bernhard lager and an offering from the tyro Matusska brewery.

The Fitzroy Tavern

16 Charlotte Street, Fitzrovia W1T 2LY

BEERS: Sam Smith's Old Brewery Bitter

Atmospheric Fitzrovia pub; its glory days may have faded into history but the prints and pictures on the walls vividly recall them

In 2001 an exhibition at the Museum of London traced the rise and fall of various artists' communities across London, from Covent Garden in the 17th century to present-day Hoxton. It demonstrated how every generation has thrown up a new set, with new ideas, in a new part of town. Longest-lived and best known of these enclaves is Fitzrovia, which took its name from a truly Bohemian pub, The Fitzroy. Fitzrovia is the area between Oxford Street and Euston Road to the south and north, and Great Portland Street and Gower Street to the west and east.

The heart of Fitzrovia, Charlotte Street, was built in 1787 and named after the hugely popular wife of the hugely unpopular King George III. The Fitzroy Coffee House was converted into a pub in 1897 and named the Hundred Marks as the neighbourood had a high proportion of German immigrants. It was renamed the Fitzroy in 1919 by publican Judah 'Pop' Kleinfeld, a Polish Russian immigrant. The street was an artists' quarter from the late 18th century to the 1950s. George Morland, an occasional lodger at The Fitzroy in 1776, can be considered Fitzrovia's first 'member'. Augustus John, who has a wall of the pub dedicated to him, was the last, dying in 1961. Other Fitzroy inhabitants included Dylan Thomas, artists' model Nina Hamnett ('Queen of Bohemia') and Tom Driberg, who in 1940 first coined the term 'Fitzrovia'.

The story of The Fitzroy is emblazoned on the walls, so there is no need to retell it here other than to point out that it is the story of a pub made great by the personality of a particular landlord. Indeed, truly great pubs are made by powerful personalities.

In the case of The Fitzroy the hero of the piece was Judah 'Pop' Kleinfeld, who took over the pub in 1919 and whose genial face can be seen in photos there today. He passed the pub to his daughter Annie, and she and her husband Charles – a man with 'mine host' features if ever there was one – ran the pub until 1956. By the 1950s The Fitzroy's spreading fame was attracting tourist trade, which gradually drove the remaining Bohemians away to a new part of town that was suitably down at heel – Soho, and with it The French House (see p.43) and the Colony Room.

We need to insert a caveat at this point. At the time of going to press the Fitrovia was shut for a refurbishment. However, this is a Sam Smith's pub, and if anyone can be relied upon to refurbish a pub faithfully and sympathetically, it is Sam Smith's. Indeed, their intention is to restore the property to as close as possible to its original design.

The French House

49 Dean Street, Soho W1 5BG

BEERS: Meteor, Guinness, Kronenbourg, Theakston's Best
(half pints only)

Famous drinking hole with a colourful past and a unique place in London's wartime history

The French House came into its own when Soho took over from Fitzrovia as the 'Bohemian' quarter of London, as The Fitzroy Tavern (see opposite) became a tourist attraction and as Soho's jazz scene started to take off. Dylan Thomas and Nina Hamnett were among those who migrated from The Fitzroy to The French House, and drinking buddies they picked up along the way included, among many others, Irish poet and playwright Brendan Behan and artist Francis Bacon.

The French House – or The French as regulars refer to it – was originally German. It was owned by a wine-shipper named Schmitt who ran it under its original name, the York Minster. In 1914 being German in London was bad for business, so the pub passed into the hands of Victor Berlemont, a colourful Belgian chef who had worked next door in the kitchens of the great Auguste Escoffier.

Maison Berlemont was a huge success, and its reputation drew international celebrities through the doors. Its fame was so widespread that during the Second World War, French speakers fleeing Hitler and craving the comfort of something familiar chose to become regulars. It became a haunt of Free French officers, and it was here that Charles de Gaulle wrote his famous rejection of the Vichy settlement: 'La France a perdu une bataille. Mais la France n'a pas perdu la guerre!' ('France has lost a battle, but France hasn't lost the war!'). On D-Day, Soho, as home to a French community for 200 years, went wild and The French House was again the centre of attention.

With the end of the war a new phase in the life of The French took place. It is said that when Victor's son, Gaston, returned from the war and walked into the pub with uniform and kit bag, Victor said, 'Oh, you're back,' gave him the keys, put his hat on and left him to it. Gaston did his father proud, and maintained The French's character and reputation. Sporting a huge moustache like his father's, Gaston became one of Soho's celebrities, noted for his generosity and charity towards his more hard-up regulars: he advanced cash to some fairly famous folk.

Gaston locked up for the last time on Bastille Day, 14 July 1989, and the pub fortunately passed into the hands of French House regulars who wanted to keep the spirit alive. Apart from a few updating alterations and an official name change from the York Minster to The French House, the pub remains much as Victor and Gaston would have remembered it. It is so full of history and character that it has had an entire book dedicated to it written by a regular; it sold out years ago, but plans for a new book are in motion.

The Guinea

30 Bruton Place, Mayfair W1J 6NL

BEERS: Young's Bitter, Young's Special, Charles Wells Bombardier

Though now particularly well-known for its award-winning steak-and-kidney pies, The Guinea was London's first 'glitterati pub', attracting the rich and famous of the 1950s

Mayfair, which takes its name from a cattle market launched by James II in 1686, is now one of London's most exclusive areas. The cattle fair was suppressed in 1730, following increasing pressure to develop on the local land. It is likely that The Guinea dates from the time of this development.

The Guinea, sometimes referred to as the 'One Pound One' (a guinea being worth £1 and one shilling in old money), was one of London's first and finest mews pubs. The pub is no longer in a mews, however, North Bruton Mews having been renamed Bruton Place in line with the area's redevelopment in the 1930s. Fortunately, the 18th-century pub survived these changes and stands alone as a piece of local history.

The pub was first referred to as The Guinea in 1755, though previous incarnations of the establishment may have included The Running Horses, The Duke's Head or The Duke of Cumberland. Dating mainly from the early 19th century, the pub passed into the Young's estate in 1888. A restaurant was added in 1953, which built such a reputation for its steaks that it earned a celebrity clientele that included Princess Margaret, Richard Burton and Elizabeth Taylor, Charlton Heston, Jack Nicklaus and Frank Sinatra. It remains a popular choice among American visitors. For those who do not want to eat in the fabulous restaurant, the bar menu includes what is arguably the world's greatest steak and kidney pie.

The pub itself is designed to cater for the peak-time, stand-up trade, being rather spartan with a tiny snug bar to one side. Plenty of dark wood surfaces and subdued lighting give the place a diffuse glow, and contribute to the pub's atmosphere of calm and egalitarian camaraderie in contrast to the reality of Mayfair outside.

The Harp

47 Chandos Place, Covent Garden WC2N 4HS

BEERS: Fuller's London Pride, Harvey's Sussex Best, Dark Star Hophead, Dark Star American Pale Ale, Sambrook's Junction, Sambrook's Wandle, plus guests

The Campaign for Real Ales' West London Pub of the Year 2008

The Harp has won many awards and is currently the Campaign for Real Ales' West London Pub of the Year. The pub was once owned by Bridget Walsh, a pioneer of real ale, and the manager believes that Walsh (along with the staff) made the pub what it is today. Once known as the Welsh Harp (though many people regard the harp as a symbol of Irish culture, it is actually more widely used in Wales as a solo instrument than in any other part of Britain), it became the plain old Harp in 1995. Close to St Martin-in-the-Fields and the frenetic rhythms of Trafalgar Square, this pub is not the place for people who want loud music or fruit machines, but it is the ideal spot to meet people and enjoy the clamour of conversation. Once office workers arrive after 5pm the Harp is often busy right up until closing time, with plenty of regulars and an occasional visit from the ENO (English National Opera company).

Inside, a long, narrow bar has an entrance at either end and is decorated with ornate mirrors together with a large number of portraits. Look out for the framed satin programme from the 1899 production of Rudyard Kipling's The Absent Minded Beggar – an interesting curiosity. Upstairs there is a cosy and comfortable function room.

Chandos Place, like many others in Covent Garden, owes its name to the Bedford family; the fourth Earl married Catherine Brydges of Chandos in 1608. Catherine's legacy is commemorated in the names of Brydges Place, Catherine Street and Chandos Street which was renamed Chandos Place in 1937.

The Lamb

92 Lamb's Conduit Street, Bloomsbury WC1N 3LZ

BEERS: Young's Bitter, Young's Special, Young's London Gold, plus guests

The Lamb has the flower baskets and well-maintained look that are characteristic of all Young's pubs and sits at the top of smart Lamb's Conduit Street.

The trouble with forcing traffic into an organically evolved place like London is that, by enabling travel at a faster speed than the streets were intended to allow, the fabric of the city is distorted. In the late 19th century it was noted that the operation of a new omnibus service frequently destroyed many of the businesses along its route. Pubs were particularly vulnerable. The damage having been done, the 21st-century traveller is still conducted down thoroughfares and directed away from the side streets and byways where, by allowing people only to travel at the city's natural pace, the best of the city manages to survive.

Take, for example, The Lamb, probably the jewel in the crown of the Young's estate. Both the pub and the semi-pedestrianized street it sits upon are named after Sir William Lamb, a gentleman of the Chapel Royal under Henry VIII. In 1577 he improved an existing conduit to bring cleaner water down to the area from Holborn. In addition he also donated 120 pails with which to carry the water from the conduit to the surrounding houses.

The pub itself was built in 1729, and though since remodelled, it is unusual in that many Victorian features remain – in particular one of the finest sets of snob screens to be found anywhere (see The Cock, p.36). The pub would have been subdivided into three or four partitions by panels that would have run from the bar to the walls. There are still clues to indicate where the panel partitions would have been. Snob screens were a product of Victorian street life, double standards and class distinction. People of different classes had to rub along together, but were very anxious that their behaviour should not be spied upon and commented on by their inferiors or superiors.

The pub also boasts an impressive collection of pictures of music-hall stars from the 1890s, all of whom performed at the now-demolished Holborn Empire, as well as pictures of actors, actresses and royalty. Reminiscent of those days, the pub even sports a working Polyphon, a very rare item. It is likely that Charles Dickens would have visited The Lamb while resident at nearby Doughty Street, where there is now a Dickens Museum. The British Museum is only a few minutes away.

LAMB AND FLAG

OSE
TREET WC2
Y OF WESTMINSTER

House LAMB & FLAG Free H

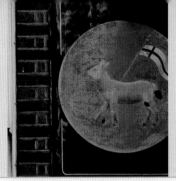

Lamb and Flag

33 Rose Street, Covent Garden WC2E 9EB

BEERS: Fuller's London Pride, Fuller's ESB, Fuller's Chiswick Bitter, Gale's Seafarers, Gale's HSB, Butcombe's Rarebreed

The Lamb and Flag is an extremely popular Covent Garden watering hole; its customers tend to spill outside in all but the very worst weather

'Meum et propositum in taberna mori vinum. Sit appositum marlentis ori, ut decunt cum venerint angelorum chori. "Deus sit propitus huic potentori".' Who could possibly disagree with such stirring sentiments as expressed on the beams of the Lamb and Flag? Perhaps you would be more inclined to concur if you knew what it meant: 'To die in a tavern is my definite plan, with my mouth to the tap as close as I can, that the angels would say, when singing began, "O Lord please show mercy to this boozy man".' Booze would appear to have fuddled the memories of those first associated with the pub, as there are conflicting claims within the building as to whether it was built in 1623, 1635 or 1638.

Taking its name from a tavern, Rose Street was built in 1623 and bore one of the earliest street signs, which simply stated, 'This is Rose St 1623' (according to some authorities) or 'Red Rose St 1623' (according to others). The area was considered particularly unsavoury throughout the 17th and 18th centuries; the poet Samuel Butler (author of *Hudibras*, a famous satire on Puritans) lived and died in the area in 1680. Lazenby Court, the low passageway to the side of the pub, was built in 1688, a few years after another poet, the rather better known John Dryden, Poet Laureate, was attacked and beaten in Rose Street in 1679, on account of some satirical lines he had written about the mistress of Charles II, the Duchess of Portsmouth. Dryden was clearly rather unlucky, for only three months later, on 18 December 1679, he was again beaten up in Rose Street, this time on

the instruction of the Earl of Rochester; and before you aver that Mr Dryden must have been a man of poor judgement, the offending lines on the latter occasion were written by someone else.

The present inn was built in 1772 and is one of only a few timber-framed buildings in central London, having survived the Great Fire of 1666, though the exterior is Georgian. Originally known as the Cooper's Arms, it was renamed the Lamb and Flag in 1883, and for some unknown reason the inn's sign is identical to the emblem of the Middle Temple Inn of Court. At one time the pub was nicknamed the Bucket of Blood, not because of the numbers of passers-by misjudging the height of Lazenby Court, but because of the prizefighting that took place there (see also The Salisbury, p.61). Charles Dickens was a frequent patron, but then he seems to have got about quite a lot.

The Nell Gwynne

1–2 Bull Inn Court, London WC2R 0NP

BEERS: St Austell Tribute, Hogs Back TEA

A hidden gem popular with locals yet only yards away from the tourist trail

That the Nell Gwynne hasn't been in previous editions of this book is a cause of eternal shame to the authors and testimony to how well kept a secret it is. A pub has been on the site since the early 1600s. It was originally called the Bull Inn – hence Bull Inn Court – and was later renamed after Charles I's famous courtesan, the actress described by Samuel Pepys as 'pretty, witty Nell': Nell Gwynne (1650–1687).

The pub has had a colourful history, as one would expect of any self-respecting Covent Garden drinking den. This has extended to very recently. The last publican but one was an ex-boxer whose customers included such East End luminaries as the Krays and the Richardsons, and for twenty years after that the publican was an ex-Playboy Bunny named Trish. Today the pub is owned by experienced operators City Pub Co. who have been careful not to touch the essential fabric of the building; and when the walls are covered in now-unobtainable original Liberty wallpaper, why would you?

This is a locals' pub. The regulars are known by name and their numbers include a fair sprinkling of actors (Pierce Brosnan shot a film there in early 2015), theatre workers and assorted celebrities who like the discrete anonymity. The staff tend to have theatrical backgrounds too. Most of the thousands of people who daily throng the Strand only yards away will never turn their feet up Bull Inn Court; consequently, those who do join the ranks of the locals will get a very warm welcome from the long-serving and loyal bar staff who take the not

unreasonable view that if you've managed to rise above the common herd and ventured within, there must be something a bit extra about you.

The pub comprises only the one smallish room, off which leads a set of death-defying stairs to the loos. A much-admired jukebox is the only modern touch and the narrow nature of Bull Inn Court means that sunlight is a rare visitor to the Nell Gwynne. The result is a wonderfully friendly and welcoming boozer, where the passage of time – like in all the best pubs – appears not to obey quite the same laws of physics as apply outside on the sunny Strand.

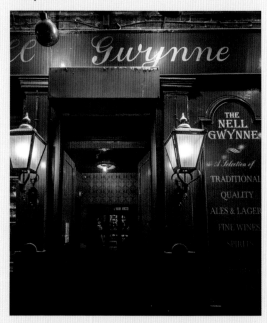

The Porterhouse

21–22 Maiden Lane, Covent Garden WC2E 7NA

BEERS: Porterhouse range

Today the superpub is all too ubiquitous, but The Porterhouse is an example of how such transformations can be done successfully: you will never be stuck for a tipple you fancy here

One look in Maiden Lane will be sufficient for you to decide that the Porterhouse is not a traditional London pub. It is, however, a great London pub for the following reasons. In recent years in high-rent locations such as Covent Garden there has been a huge increase in competition for the money of Londoners and tourists alike. The 'superpub', i.e. one capable of absorbing around 500 people, is merely the latest manifestation in this on-going struggle, and Covent Garden and Leicester Square have seen an explosion in the number of superpubs. The majority of these establishments lack character and atmosphere; the exception is The Porterhouse.

This superpub works because of its attention to detail and quality. The Porterhouse is vast, but deceptively so. It is split into many levels, so you always feel you are in a rather smaller space than is actually the case. The varying levels are further broken up to create alcoves and intimate spaces. The usual decoration is case after case of bottled beer. There must be a couple of thousand bottles on display, and one does not need to be a beer aficionado to realize that this is a truly impressive global collection, reminiscent of the days when London pubs frequently did house huge collections of the weird and wonderful (see The Churchill Arms, p.159).

The next thing you quickly notice in this award-winning interior is the amount of copper. The contents of a small mine have been extracted and worked into banisters, chair backs, pipes, footrests and flues to create a warm glow throughout.

There are even copper clocks and anglepoise lamps. Finally, the third thing one notices is The Porterhouse's own beers: they are all imported from the brewery of the same name in Dublin, and the beers are as diverse as they are carefully crafted. They are also totally unavailable elsewhere in London. A genuine Irish pub, therefore, so good *craic* is guaranteed.

Princess Louise

208 High Holborn, Holborn WC1V 7BW

BEERS: Sam Smith's Taddy Lager, Sam Smith's Pure Brewed Organic Lager, Sam Smith's Double Four Lager, Sam Smith's Alpine Lager, Sam Smith's Old Brewery Bitter

The plain exterior of this pub gives little clue as to what is inside

The Princess Louise retains the finest, most complete, most original, best preserved, most authentic high-Victorian pub interior in London. It is a national treasure. It is rumoured that even the gents' toilets – by J. Tylor & Sons of London & Sydney no less – are Grade II listed and, gentlemen, once you have paid them a visit other urinals will seem mean by comparison.

The spectacular thing about the Princess is the degree of craftsmanship displayed on almost every surface. What is often forgotten today is the extent to which our late great Victorian 'gin palace'-style pubs were not just opulent because opulence was the fashion, they were opulent because they could afford to be. To truly understand the Princess Louise, and the other great pub interiors of the time, you need to understand that they were also a statement of nationhood. The pub was built in 1872,

named after a daughter of Queen Victoria, and was remodelled in 1891 to more or less its present form. It was very much a pub of its day, and its day was the height of the British Empire, when Britain was home to a very proud race who happened to be running the largest empire the world had ever seen. Britain was also the 'workshop of the world', its craftsmen were the best in the world, and the Victorians liked to be reminded of this. R. Morris Ltd of 293 Kennington Road, south-east London, were so proud of the beautiful mirrors they produced for the Princess Louise that they signed them.

A glance at the rich lincrusta ceiling indicates that the pub was previously subdivided with a narrow corridor along the side – much like The Argyll Arms (see p.30) – and the comparison of these two pubs is a useful reminder that the Princess Louise was once unexceptional. Sadly, what the Luftwaffe did not destroy brewery accountants set out to. In many cases they were rather more successful than the Luftwaffe. The Princess survives as much by luck as by judgement, as what is a wonder to one generation can seem mundane to another – incredibly it does not warrant much mention in the pub guides of the 1960s, other than a passing note that it was a popular venue for folk music in the 1950s.

The pub also serves a range of starters like soup, nachos and garlic bread, food such as Chicken & Wiltshire Ham Pie and Macaroni Cheese as well as assorted fish dishes, burgers, hotdogs, sandwiches, salads, and sides, and desserts including Belgian Waffles and Sticky Toffee Pudding.

The Queens Larder

1 Queen Square, Bloomsbury WC1N 3AR

BEERS: Greene King IPA, Redemption Hopspur, plus 2 guest ales

The Queens Larder is a reminder that our pubs and their names are all part of the nation's history; this one serves a secluded and very attractive corner of the city and offers a lovely ambience

The pub now known as The Queens Larder is known to have existed in 1720 as a humble alehouse without a sign. Later in the century, George III, who was to become the longest reigning monarch since Henry III, started to show signs of the mental illness with which the modern public is so familiar following the success of the play and film about him.

During the initial period of his illness, when news of his incapacity was too sensitive to be made public – and indeed the nature of his illness was not understood – the king was confined in Queen Square at the home of his physician Dr Willis. The king's wife, Queen Charlotte, rented a small cellar under the alehouse in which secretly to store delicacies and provisions that might relieve the tedium and misery of the king's confinement. Queen Square is not named after her, but after Queen Anne, who died in 1712 while the square was being built (1708–20); there is, however, a statue of Queen Charlotte in the square, although this has nothing to do with recognition of her compassion towards her husband, as it was erected between 1775 and 1780 and his first confinement was not until 1788–9.

George III had one further period of severe mental instability in 1801 and finally became deranged in 1810, occasioning his hugely unpopular and much less cultured son to act as Regent until the king's death in 1820. As a consequence of her devotion to her husband, the pub was renamed The Queens Larder once the facts of the matter had entered the public domain.

Queen Square has always been something of a centre for philanthropy and medicine. The Foundling Hospital was next to the square in Guildford Street, founded in 1742 by Captain Thomas Coram who was frequently appalled by the sight of small children exposed in the streets, abandoned by their parents and 'left

to die in dung hills'. After 17 years' work among these children he persuaded 21 ladies of nobility and distinction to petition the king, and in 1739 a Royal Charter was granted for The Hospital for the Maintenance and Education of Exposed and Deserted Young Children. Coram numbered among his benefactors many of the great and good, who were enthused by the success of this remarkable institution. Hogarth helped provide decorations for the Court Room of the hospital, as did Gainsborough and Reynolds. In 1749 Handel wrote the *Foundling Hospital Anthem* as a fundraiser. The Great Ormond Street Hospital for Sick Children is also just off Queen Square.

The Red Lion

Crown Passage, Pall Mall SW1Y 6PP

BEERS: Adnams Bitter, St Austell Tribute

A charming, friendly pub that holds the second oldest licence in London

The Red Lion is one of London's great establishments. It is true that the clubs of Pall Mall, St James's Palace, Clarence House, and the exclusive shops on St James's Street are all grander, but whether they are more important is open to debate. For a start, without the customers of The Red Lion none of these other establishments could operate. The clientele comprises the chefs and doormen of the clubs, the hatters and wine merchants of St James, the royal protection officers from the palaces. It also comprises gentlemen popping in for a beer before moving on to stuffier surroundings, or the clients of the said hatters and wine merchants, and all the while The Red Lion is one of the most egalitarian and companionable pubs in London. There is a fair sprinkling of tourists, who have heard about it from other tourists with the words 'If you visit just one pub...'

If you were to list all the people who had popped into The Red Lion to pass an idle few minutes and had left hours later with a new band of lifelong friends it would run into the thousands. It is a totally magical and very happy place. At least 330 years old, it is the holder of the second oldest licence in London. It proudly claims to be London's oldest village inn, and if you visit the small first-floor lounge you can experience the basis of this claim: it is charming and makes you forget you are in London.

In its heyday the pub was a 'wenching house', and recent restoration unearthed a mysterious glass panel set into a floor which could only have been used for voyeuristic purposes (which may also explain the early licence, as influential patrons

often sought to safeguard their recreation). There are, allegedly, secret passages leading to St James's Palace, although this seems unlikely if you study the local geography. The pub is certainly in what was one of the most rakish parts of London. The courtyard of nearby Berry Bros & Rudd wine merchants was the scene of London's last legal duel. The loser breathed his last on the floor of The Red Lion. More refined patrons have included actor Pierce Brosnan, who used the pub while filming scenes at the nearby Reform Club for the James Bond film *Die Another Day*.

The Red Lion

2 Duke of York Street, St James's SW1Y 6JP

BEERS: Fuller's London Pride, Timothy Taylor Landlord, Hook Norton Old Hooky, plus guests

A survivor of the Blitz, this pub is an excellent reminder of the style of pub that would once have littered the streets of central London

Is there anything truly extraordinary about The Red Lion to earn it the accolade of being London's most photographed pub interior? If there is, no one really seems to know what it is. An obvious reason behind its fame is undoubtedly its magnificent decoration, but that is only part of the story, and the main reason for its fame is simply its survival. Without wishing to sound too glib, the reason why it has survived is that it has not been destroyed, and it has not been destroyed because no one has managed to drop a bomb on it. Part of The Red Lion's appeal, therefore, is as a reminder of the hundreds of fine pubs that did not survive either the Blitz, road-widening initiatives, slum clearances or redevelopments.

The Red Lion was built, as its Georgian façade suggests, in 1821, on the site of an earlier pub, as was common, and it was remodelled in the 1870s, which was equally common. Evidence of the remodelling work can be found in the varying styles of glasswork, for which the pub is famous – that in the doors and partitions is earlier than that in the ornate mirrors. The mirrors, which may have been crafted by Walter Gibbs and Sons of Blackfriars, cover nearly every wall surface and are the product of later improvements in the techniques of engraving and etching. Some believe that the reason behind such an abundance of mirrors was an initiative by magistrates to reduce the privacy of the snugs and thereby reduce the chances of casual prostitution taking place in the pub.

The pub is small and this serves to remind us that in its heyday its clientele, though numerous, would probably only have been inclined, or able, to stay for shorter periods – popping in and out would have been the norm. The pub would nevertheless have been a bustling centre of activity and information, and a focus for the scandal and gossip emanating from the grand houses and clubs of St James.

Nearby attractions include the London Library, the Royal Academy, Fortnum and Mason's, and the shops of Jermyn Street. St James's Piccadilly, a church designed by Sir Christopher Wren and a popular concert venue, is only 20 yards away.

The Red Lion

48 Parliament Street, Whitehall SW1A 2NH

BEERS: Fuller's range plus guest

The politicians' pub, the Red Lion played a role in carving out the destiny of New Labour in the early 1990s

There is a lake in Wales into which, according to legend, a stream flows in and out without ever mixing with the waters of the lake. The Red Lion in Parliament Street is a bit like that. A constant stream of tourists pass through this narrow Westminster pub, never to return, while a dedicated band of regulars returns day in and day out. A third group consists of those who have finished their day's business in the Palace of Westminster, Downing Street or the Treasury, and wish to ponder the success or otherwise of their mission.

Many who fall into the latter two groups are likely to have known the former landlord Raoul de Vere, who is now retired. A former policeman, he was a pioneer of the Pubwatch scheme of pub/police co-operation and an industry figure whose opinion was frequently sought by legislators. The pub itself is directly opposite the Treasury building, which was designed by the impressive architectural trio of William Kent, Sir John Soane and Sir Charles Barry and completed in 1845.

The Red Lion is also a few doors down from the house of Sir George Burke, a friend of Isambard Kingdom Brunel, who lodged directly across the street. Brunel ran a piece of string attached to a bell across the street in order to summon his friend to the window so he could telegraph messages to him or beckon him to go for an early morning walk.

The pub sports a rather lopsided aspect – it is long and narrow and the bar runs along one wall beneath the stairs up to the dining room, which gained notoriety in the early 1990s as a place where Labour modernizers gathered to hatch New Labour. The pictures on the walls are very much of a political nature. When the metropolitan police were in Scotland Yard it was very much their pub. Charles Dickens was also familiar with The Red Lion – he used it as the inn where David Copperfield asked for 'a glass of Genuine Stunning' ale and was given it with a kiss; this has earned him a bust high up in the wall. Geoffrey Chaucer is also honoured with a bust, but since there has only been a pub on the site since 1437, it is impossible that he would ever have supped here.

The pub was refurbished recently; the cellar bar is now called The Cabinet Room, and has been decorated in the style of the old gin bars.

The Salisbury

90 St Martin's Lane, Strand WC2N 4AP

BEERS: Young's Bitter, Timothy Taylor Landlord, Deuchars IPA, Charles Wells Bombardier, plus guests

The Salisbury boasts one of the most flamboyant and high-Victorian interiors of all London pubs

One of central London's most spectacular pub interiors belongs to a pub with quite a history. At one time The Salisbury was known as the Coach & Horses, then it became the Ben Caunt's Head after a landlord who enjoyed celebrity as a bare-knuckle fighter (aka the Nottinghamshire Giant). In the early 19th century it was well known as a venue for pugilistic contests, notably the return from retirement of Jim Belcher to face 'the Game Chicken' – sadly, history does not record the result.

In 1892 a new lease was taken out on the property from the Marquis of Salisbury, a favourite of Queen Victoria and a direct descendant of Robert Cecil, the first Earl of Salisbury (a favourite of Queen Elizabeth I). The marquis was a good friend of public houses too. When Temperance campaigners argued that a reduction in the number of pubs would lead to a reduction in drunkenness his lordship replied that he could not follow the logic of their argument; after all, he said, he owned an awful lot of bedrooms but he did not find that that led to him sleeping more. The pub was already known as The Salisbury Stores, which would indicate that it acted as a wine merchant's as well as a gin palace.

The pub was rebuilt in 1898, and it is this magnificent interior that we are fortunate enough to enjoy today; although the pub was restored in 1963, it was done in the most sympathetic manner. Being located in the heart of Theatreland the pub has enjoyed a great many theatrical connections. In the days when homosexuality was a criminal offence, it was something of a haven for London's theatrical gay community. In the 1960s, when 'Stores' was dropped

from its name, it enjoyed a vogue as 'the actors' pub'. These days it is more likely to be full of audiences now that the days of celebrity and paparazzi make a relaxed drink impossible for stars. The pub was used as a location in the 1961 Dirk Bogarde film *The Victim*.

The Salisbury is ideally situated for refreshment before or after engaging in a wide variety of nearby entertainment. There is opera to be had at the Coliseum and candlelit concerts at St Martin-in-the-Fields. Famous faces are to be seen at the National Portrait Gallery and the brushstrokes of old masters can be examined in the National Gallery. And, of course, there are always the theatres.

The Seven Stars

53 Carey Street, Holborn WC2A 2JB

BEERS: Whistable, Sharp's Cornish Coaster, Sambrook's Brewery, Adnams Bitter

Political humour dating back to the battles between Whigs and Tories sits alongside film posters on the walls of this busy pub

The Seven Stars is an outpost of Soho and a city institution in its own right. The pub is said to have been built in 1602 and survived the Great Fire of London of 1666, though how much of the present fabric of the building is original is open to debate. Nevertheless, a rustic feel pervades this simple pub.

It is reported to have originally been named the League of Seven Stars after the seven provinces that make up the Netherlands, on account of the fact that Dutch sailors were reputed to have settled in the neighbourhood. If the Dutch did have a presence here they have left precious little sign of it elsewhere in the vicinity. Also departed from the neighbourhood, and very nearly forgotten, are the bankruptcy courts, from the days when

bankruptcy was an offence and bankrupts – such as Charles Dickens's father – would find themselves in debtors' prisons such as the Marshalsea in Southwark (Dickens set *Little Dorritt* around the Marshalsea and was familiar with The Seven Stars). To be in Carey Street, the street on which the pub stands, was once a London euphemism for being 'brassic', 'skint' or 'broke' – all good London terms, too.

Today the pub is entirely surrounded by London's legal community. The rear of the Royal Courts of Justice provides the view from the pub doorway, while Lincoln's Inn, one of the four Inns of Court, is to the rear. They are referred to as 'inns' in the same way that a pub may be an inn, as they both derive from the old English word for a chamber. One attraction of this visually striking pub is the landlady, the exotically named Roxy Beaujolais. A quick perusal of the walls will enable you to ascertain that she is very much a figure in the London pub scene, and astute readers may be able to work out who she is sitting next to in the photo captioned 'Three Greyhounds 1996'.

Those fortunate enough not to have business at either the Royal Courts of Justice or Lincoln's Inn might have time to visit the Soane Museum on the north side of Lincoln's Inn Fields, the former house of the architect Sir John Soane, designer of the Dulwich Picture Gallery. Alternatively, you could walk through Lincoln's Inn to Chancery Lane and the London Silver Vaults, one of London's great hidden treasures – literally.

The Ship & Shovell

1–3 Craven Passage, Strand WC2N 5PH

BEERS: Badger First Call, Tanglefoot, King and Barnes Sussex

This is the only pub in London with two frontages that face each other

The novelist and writer on London, Peter Ackroyd, likes to think of London as a living organism, an entity with a spirit brought to life by 2,000 years of human activity on one spot. In the oldest parts of London, as in Ackroyd's beloved Clerkenwell, that spirit is almost tangible; there are eddies and currents in the city that defy the zeitgeist. Starbucks and McDonalds may shape the look of modern London, but away from the homogenized high streets lies the old city, shaped by the deep, subliminal nature of Londoners.

Take, for example, The Ship & Shovell. Located just behind Charing Cross Station and the Embankment, it is a few tantalizing paces from thronging Villiers Street, yet is a mystery to all but a handful of the thousands of scurrying figures who daily pass within 50 yards of it. The pub was established around 1740, but sadly lay derelict between 1981 and 1996, when it was renovated and restored by the present owners. They tired of the view opposite, which was of another derelict property, and took it over, connected the two beneath the pavement of Crown Passage and opened it as a half-pub in 1999. It is now unique as the only pub with two frontages facing each other.

The pub takes its name from Admiral Sir Cloudesley Shovell (1650–1707) who, like Nelson, joined the navy at the age of 13, rising to earn a commission – an exceptional feat at a time when most were purchased. Prior to his appointment as Admiral of the Fleet, he lived at nearby May Place. His career highlight came with the capture of Gibraltar and his promotion to Commander in Chief of the English Fleet. Sadly, this exalted position was his downfall, for in 1707 his flagship, HMS *Association*, foundered off the Scilly Isles and, as he struggled ashore, he was strangled by a local woman desperate to steal his emerald ring.

Star & Garter

62 Poland Street, Soho W1F 7NX

BEERS: Fuller's London Pride, Shepherd Neame Spitfire, Greene King IPA

A no-frills, honest-to-goodness local in the heart of Soho, which makes a welcome reprieve from the showiness that often dominates the area

The Star & Garter has had the very good fortune of having been left well alone by modern tastes, and the result is a Soho pub that is not trying to make a statement, or trying too hard to attract a certain crowd. Appearing in Poland Street as the Star & Garter in around 1825, the pub takes its name from the badge of the Order of the Garter, one of the highest remaining chivalric orders in the United Kingdom, along with the Order of the Bath.

A fine mirror bearing the star and garter forms the focus of the pub. The garter bears the motto of the British monarchy, which dates back to the days of Edward III, who in 1348 first uttered the words 'Honi soit qui mal y pense' – 'Evil be to he that thinks it'. According to legend, at a ball, possibly held at Calais, Joan Countess of Salisbury dropped her garter and King Edward, seeing her embarrassment, picked it up and bound it about his own leg saying in French, 'Evil (or shamed) be he that thinks evil of it'; however, this is almost certainly a later fiction. It is much more likely that the device was a small strap, possibly used to attach pieces of armour, and was used as a symbol of binding together in common brotherhood; the motto probably refers to the leading political topic of the 1340s, Edward's claim to the throne of France.

Poland Street began life in the 1680s and building continued until about 1707. It takes its name from a pub originally called the King of Poland, which was known as the Dickens Wine House when it was destroyed by a bomb in 1940. The street's most famous resident was William Blake, who lends his name to the Star & Garter's upstairs bar. Blake lived at No. 28 from 1785 to 1791, and was a neighbour of Elizabeth Billington, who, being the mistress of both the Duke of Rutland and the Prince of Wales, must have been quite a beauty. Those being the days when everyone in London knew everyone's business, she was disapprovingly known as the 'Poland Street Man Trap'.

THE CITY &
THE EAST END

Many pubs in London are great survivors, and none more so than those of the City and the East End, where whole swaths of land were left desolate by the Blitz and then depersonalized by post-war developments. In recent years, there has been something of a revival of these areas and their communities, and as a result more people are discovering the great pubs that have shaped the character of the area through hard times and good times. Whatever your mood, you'll find a pub to please, as there is everything here, from traditional East End boozers, such as The Pride of Spitalfields, to the jaw-dropping elaborate décor of The Black Friar, to secluded establishments such as Ye Olde Mitre Tavern.

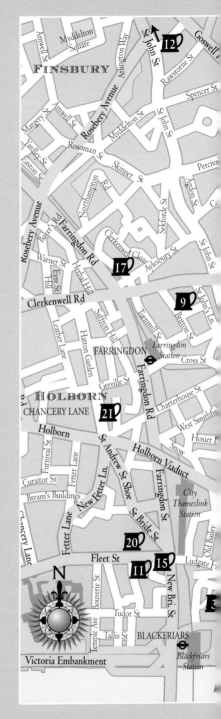

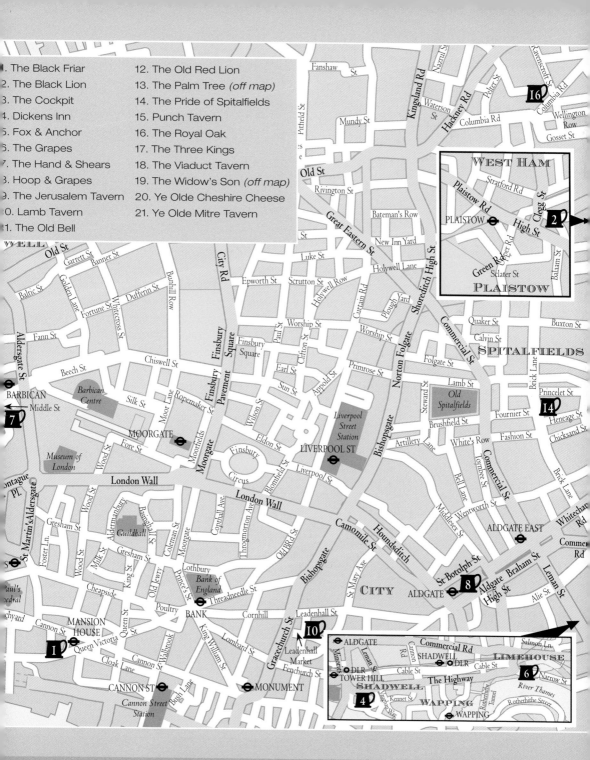

1. The Black Friar
2. The Black Lion
3. The Cockpit
4. Dickens Inn
5. Fox & Anchor
6. The Grapes
7. The Hand & Shears
8. Hoop & Grapes
9. The Jerusalem Tavern
10. Lamb Tavern
11. The Old Bell

12. The Old Red Lion
13. The Palm Tree (off map)
14. The Pride of Spitalfields
15. Punch Tavern
16. The Royal Oak
17. The Three Kings
18. The Viaduct Tavern
19. The Widow's Son (off map)
20. Ye Olde Cheshire Cheese
21. Ye Olde Mitre Tavern

The Black Friar

174 Queen Victoria Street, Blackfriars EC4V 4EG

BEERS: Nicholson's Pale Ale, Sharp's Doom Bar, Truman's Runner, plus 5 guests

London's only true Art Nouveau public house, the Black Friar is unique for its elaborate interior

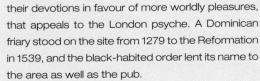

The staggering fact one learns on a visit to The Black Friar is that it was due for demolition in the 1960s. Today it is a Grade I listed building, but it took a public outcry to save this unique pub from the wrecker's ball. The Black Friar holds a special place of affection in Londoners' hearts – it is so completely over the top that you cannot but fall in love with it. There is something naughty about the images of rotund, jovial friars, seemingly neglecting their devotions in favour of more worldly pleasures, that appeals to the London psyche. A Dominican friary stood on the site from 1279 to the Reformation in 1539, and the black-habited order lent its name to the area as well as the pub.

It is amazing that the pub exists at all: it was built in 1902–04 in an Anglicized Art Nouveau style at a time when the London pub market had crashed and bankruptcies were many times more common than new building works. Consequently, there are very few London pubs dating from this era (see also The Coal Hole, pp.34–35), and those that survive are wonderfully idiosyncratic. The narrow end of the building assumes a mock baronial hall style, which gives over to a sumptuous and intimate room at the back that defies analogy. Friezes in copper and plaster by Henry Poole RA depicting monks having a good time hover above signs offering such pearls of wisdom as 'finery is foolery', or 'don't advertise, tell a gossip'. There are upwards of 50 different types of marble employed in the building, which, with authentic Art Nouveau light fittings, furniture and wood carving lends the whole an air that – a preponderance of cowls and habits notwithstanding – tempts one to feel rather indulgent.

The sign over the partition between the two parts of the bar suggests that this site was where the Holy Roman Emperor Charles V, the Papal Legate and Henry VIII all met in 1532 to discuss the dissolution of Henry's marriage to Catherine of Aragon. It is not hard to imagine the bluff King Henry propping up the bar, though the sight of him would wipe the smiles from the faces of the jolly monks.

The Black Lion

Plaistow High Street, Plaistow E13 0AD

BEERS: Rotating, including Courage Best, Mighty Oak, Captain Bob, Doom Bar, Broadside, Landlord

Everyone from legendary highwayman Dick Turpin to the footballing legend Bobby Moore has drunk at this down-to-earth East End pub.

Originally built over 600 years ago, The Black Lion was reconstructed about 280 years ago. Many features of the early coaching inn remain, such as the cobbled coaching yard. The pub is extensive, and is a good example of how we have forgotten about many of the ancillary functions that such houses used to provide and which required a depth of property much greater than just a front bar, which is all that so many of us see in a pub today. Go through to the coaching yard, which is defended by a stout oak gate, and you will see the old stables area, now converted into a function room. Part of the former coaching yard is now a beer garden.

The Black Lion retained a boxing association for 93 years of its history. The West Ham Boys Boxing Club trained in a hall to the left of the courtyard, though the gym has now moved away. It was home to Terry Spinks, the first Briton to win an Olympic boxing gold, at the 1956 Games; George Walker, creator of the Brent Walker pubs and clubs empire, trained here with his brother Billy; while champion prize-fighters Barry McGuigan and Nigel Benn both worked out at The Black Lion. Sporting connections do not end with boxing: the 1966 World Cup England captain, Bobby Moore, was a regular.

Inside the pub you are transported to the countryside. Low ceilings, wood floors, oak beams, bare brick walls adorned with brewery ephemera acquired over generations all give the impression of a rural inn. Several generations are well represented here. There have been only six landlords since 1929, and Milly Morris, a famous East End barmaid,

served behind the bar from 1929 until 1997. She was able to regale customers with tales about the pub during the Second World War when the cellars were used as air-raid shelters. Evidence of the shelters is still to be seen, although no longer visible are the smugglers' tunnels which extend over half a mile to emerge very close to the Upton Park football ground, and with which the notorious highwayman Dick Turpin may well have been familiar – he used to stable Black Bess in what is now the function room.

The Cockpit

7 St Andrews Hill, Blackfriars EC4V 5BY

BEERS: Courage Best and Directors, Theakston's Old Peculiar

A traditional Victorian exterior conceals a mock-Tudor interior; this is a true East End pub sat within the City walls and a reminder of the community that predates the City's role as a financial centre

The Cockpit is a bit out of place in EC4, as it looks much more like an East End boozer than a City one; but this is its charm – it even opens on a Sunday. Dating from the 16th century, it may well have been familiar to William Shakespeare. It was originally known as The Cock Pit (as two words), and cockfighting was one of its main activities and attractions. When cockfighting was banned in 1849 the pub's name changed to The Three Castles (one of which would have been for Baynard's Castle, a Norman fortress that stood at the foot of St Andrew's Hill until the Great Fire of 1666). Refurbishment of the pub in the 1970s saw the introduction of a spectators' gallery around the first-floor interior and the restoration of The Cockpit name.

The Cockpit is also the proud owner of a rare shove-ha'penny board – ask behind the bar for the necessary old pennies, and there will be no shortage of willing locals offering to show you how to play.

Just as the 2,000 year-old City is ever changing, The Cockpit reminds you that there are aspects of it that stay remarkably constant. The Londoner is one of these, and The Cockpit is a Londoner's pub. Many customers today will be direct descendants of those who went to watch the bird fights in centuries past, and are drawn from the invisible City – the one that does not draw large salaries or award itself fat bonuses, but provides all the services and necessities for the one that does.

This is why the pub opens on a Sunday, because many of its customers have to work on Sunday too. For this reason it is popular with the bell ringers of St Paul's Cathedral; it is also open on Good Friday. If you should find yourself in the City on a Sunday, which will be more likely now that the Millennium Bridge is open to ferry people from the Tate Modern to St Paul's Cathedral, it is worth remembering that The Cockpit is probably the only pub you will find open between the Embankment and Liverpool Street.

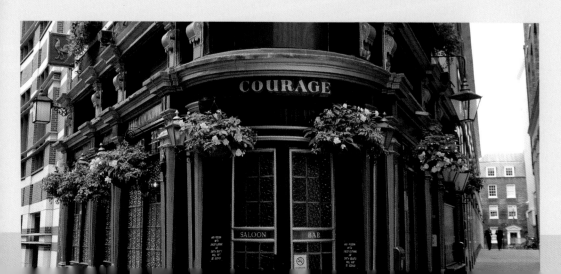

Dickens Inn

St Katharine's Dock, Tower Hill E1W 1UH

BEERS: Tribute, Green King IPA, Adnams

The tranquil surroundings of St Katharine's Dock make The Dickens Inn a good place for refreshment along the riverside

Dickens Inn was originally a brewery building dating from the 18th century that was later used as a spice warehouse. Then, some 25 years ago, it was painstakingly relocated, timber by timber, to the exclusive St Katharine's Dock. For those with an interest in construction, photographs of the meticulous process are on display. Despite its age, fans of Charles Dickens should note that, beyond its new location, there is no connection between the building, the pub or the prolific novelist.

St Katharine's Dock itself opened in 1828, having been designed and built in an impressively speedy two years by the engineer Thomas Telford of canal- and bridge-building fame to create extra capacity for London's overstretched port space. The spoil from the excavations was carted off to Belgrave Square (see The Star Tavern, p.112), and the resultant dock specialized in cargoes such as ivory and spices. Bomb damage in the last war ended St Katharine's commercial history. It fell into disuse, and the local pubs also suffered as London's port trade contracted to the Isle of Dogs and the Royal Docks.

The docks' warehouses have since been converted into luxury apartments and shops, and many fine yachts of the rich and famous can be spotted in the marina.

Dickens Inn opened in 1976 in 'the style of a 19th century balconied two storied inn' (sic), despite the fact that according to the history books there never was such a thing and that it is actually three storeys. The timber construction makes it one of the more unusual pubs in London, and it is a large, loud and fun place to drink. Each floor offers something different in the way of food, becoming more expensive as you climb up the stairs – bar food, pizza restaurant and finally an expensive restaurant on the top floor. Dickens Inn is a good place to start or finish a riverside walk or from which to enjoy the Tower of London and the many attractions south of Tower Bridge.

Fox & Anchor

115 Charterhouse Street, Clerkenwell EC1M 6AA

BEERS: Young's Bitter, Young's Special, Young's Stout, plus guests

Hops, chops, cuvees and duvets, so says the sign; perfectly kept real ales served in pewter mugs round off this glorious pub

Tucked into Charterhouse Street in one of the very oldest parts of London, The Fox & Anchor enjoys that supreme imprimatur of excellence that can be only gained and never awarded – recognition.

Once, when London pubs had restricted opening hours, the Fox had a special licence that enabled it to open early in the morning and serve breakfast to workers at nearby Smithfield Market. It is still open early but in recent years its owners have stylishly restored it with mahogany doors, etched glass and heavy brass. The Fox exudes class and style; its embossed ceilings testify to its Victorian origins. It is gloriously gastronomic, serving great food at attractive prices, and thankfully local. There is also a superb range of perfectly kept real ales.

A sign says the pub offers hops, chops, cuvees and duvets. The duvets come not in the bar but in the six bedrooms that have recently been opened. Each is different and features works by local artists.

The Fox is a handsome specimen, and was the winner of the English Heritage/CAMRA Restoration Award in 1993. The pub's subdued lighting is reminiscent of the days when it would have been gas lit, and the small collapsible shelf running the length of the wall opposite the bar conjures up times past when many meals would have been eaten standing up by people in rather more haste than you are likely to be.

The pub is next to Charterhouse Square, once home to a Carthusian monastery, and from which Charterhouse School takes its name. Suttons Hospital is a survival of the monastery, and the brothers run pre-arranged tours of this alms establishment, which was used by Elizabeth I prior to her coronation. On the opposite side of the square is Florin Court, a fine piece of Art Deco architecture that was used as the exterior of Hercule Poirot's apartments in the television series.

The pub was formerly a free house but is now a managed house by Young's Brewery.

The Grapes

76 Narrow Street, Limehouse E14 8BP

BEERS: Adnams Bitter, Timothy Taylor Landlord, Marston's Pedigree, plus guests

Whether you just want a quick pint or a blow-out meal at the noted fish restaurant upstairs, a welcoming ambience permeates the whole pub

Records show a hostelry on the site of The Grapes in the 16th century, and the present building goes back to a very creditable 1650. One of East London's best known pubs, it is also a noted fish restaurant. The first-floor dining room is known as The Dickens Room in honour of the fact that Charles Dickens is supposed to have used The Grapes as the model for the Six Jolly Fellowship Porters in Our Mutual Friend, though there are other riverside pubs – The Prospect of Whitby, for example – that have also claimed this over the years.

A guidebook of 1968 notes that the 'atmosphere is surprisingly cosmopolitan; there are seamen and dockers, tourists and visitors and locals.' Well, the seamen and dockers have gone as the warehouses roundabouts have all been turned into luxury apartments, but The Grapes retains its cosmopolitan atmosphere. This long, narrow pub

is divided into two by the staircase to The Dickens Room. A small balcony, sheltered by high-sided wooden screens, allows for stunning views of the ever-changing River Thames, and the equally ever-changing skyline of the Isle of Dogs.

The décor theme is a mixture of Dickensian London and old East End London, plus some river ephemera, all in tastefully subdued tones as is proper for a London pub. Though the inevitable wear and tear has been seen to, The Grapes benefits from not having received too much attention over the years, unlike some of its riverside neighbours.

The Grapes is a great stopping point during an amble along the river, and if you prefer your water rather slower moving than the turbulent Thames then Limehouse Basin, where the Regent's Canal meets the river, is only a short walk away.

The Hand & Shears

1 Middle Street, Smithfield EC1A 7JA

BEERS: Timothy Taylor Landlord, Sharp's Doom Bar, plus 4 guests

The imposing inn sign refers to the cloth fair that took place outside the doors of the pub in medieval times – or, as jokers would have it, to the practices of the surgeons at nearby St Bartholomew's Hospital

This handsome corner pub was built in 1849, but stands on the site of earlier taverns dating back to the 12th century. Set in the precincts of St Bartholomew's Priory, it was ideally suited to act as the focal point for the cloth fair that took place there and which lent its name to the nearby street. This was held here every year for a fortnight commencing upon St Bartholomew's Day, 24 August. The first cloth fair took place in 1133 and in subsequent years assumed increasing importance, so that traders travelled from all over Europe. As is the way of the City it fell to the guilds to regulate trade in their craft, and by the 16th century it was the job of the Merchant Taylors' Company – first chartered in 1327 – to police the fair. Their official would patrol the fair with a silver standard yard rule to ensure that the City's bylaws and ordinances were upheld. Transgressors were 'tried' at The Hand & Shears, and the usual punishment was a period in the stocks or a flogging. This tradition led to a growing association between the guild and the tavern, so much so that the tavern was allowed to use the Merchant Taylor's badge as its inn sign. Today a stylized version of shears cutting silken cloth is painted over the door.

The last cloth fair was opened by the Lord Mayor of London from the steps of the pub in 1855. Some time before this the principal association of the pub had shifted from cloth cutting to shroud wearing. Newgate Prison was nearby (the site is now the Old Bailey Central Criminal Courts), and when executions were still performed outside its walls, the Hand & Shears was the traditional stop for the condemned man to receive his last drop before the last drop.

Charles Dickens was a vociferous campaigner against public executions, and after a multiple execution on the roof of the Horsemonger Lane gaol in 1849 he told a friend that he 'felt for some time afterwards almost as if I were living in a city of devils'. In 1868, within Dickens' lifetime, executions in public ceased. Incidentally, it was in 1849, with the construction of the present pub building, that the last-drink custom ceased at the Hand & Shears.

London wags also quip that the Hand & Shears is a reference to the abilities or lack of them of the surgeons of St Bartholomew's Hospital, since these gentlemen are also known to frequent the pub – hence the number of cartoons of a medical theme on the walls.

Hoop & Grapes

47 Aldgate High Street, Aldgate EC3N 1AL

BEERS: Nicholson's Pale Ale, Sharp's Doom Bar, plus guests

The Hoop & Grapes is a historic treasure chest, having seen armies, monarchs and most of London pass before its ancient timber frame

One of London's most historic inns, the Hoop & Grapes also has one of the best documented histories of any London pub. When it was built in 1598 it took the name The Castle. It is an exceptional building for a number of reasons: it was built of imported softwood, a consequence of the shortage of domestic hardwoods (cooperage was a major drain on hardwood supplies, to the extent that in the mid-16th century Queen Mary had to put a limit on the size of cask used for export).

It survived the Great Conflagration in 1666, and is now the only timber-framed building left in the City, as timber frames were subsequently banned for buildings in order to prevent further devastating fires. Although the building was substantially restored in 1983, the repairers were sensitive to the fact that in 400 years the pub had shifted slightly – some 18 inches in fact, and perhaps it is this 'out of kilter' nature of the building that is its greatest charm.

Aldgate, or 'old gate', was one of London's key thoroughfares and is its most historic. It was one of the six Roman entrances to London. In 1215 the barons came through it to force King John to sign the Magna Carta. Chaucer leased the room over the gate itself between 1374 and 1385. In 1471, during the Wars of the Roses, 5,000 men under the command of the Bastard of Fauconberg were routed when they demanded entry and the Aldgate portcullis was lowered behind them. Mary Tudor entered London here for the first time as Queen; Princess Elizabeth met her with a 2,000-strong guard of honour. The gate was demolished in 1761.

Aldgate being just on the borders of the City, traders could supply the City's needs without the fines and fees that accompanied commerce within the City walls. As is usual, various trades gathered in different quarters, and Aldgate became associated with butchers. The area was known as Butchers' Row, it being easier to slaughter animals outside the City walls than in the cramped conditions within. The Hoop & Grapes straddled the borders of the City, being simultaneously in the parish wards of St Botolph Aldgate and St Mary Whitechapel. The ward boundary marker plates are still clearly visible on the party wall to the right of the pub door.

The Jerusalem Tavern

55 Britton Street, Clerkenwell EC1M 5UQ

BEERS: St Peter's Brewery full range

This 'modern' pub has recreated a lost 18th-century atmosphere and style very convincingly; it is also renowned for the unique range of microbrewery beers it serves

The Jerusalem Tavern is one of the most authentic-looking 18th-century tavern-style pubs in London. This is a great tribute to its owners, St Peter's Brewery of Suffolk, and their award-winning architect – for it is, in fact, no such thing. The brewery actually created the tavern from a fine 1720 townhouse that was formerly a coffee shop and then a tea room, and it is blessed with a great atmosphere.

The windows date from c.1840, and the provenance of the dairy-style blue and white tiles on the front walls, which add so much to the feel of the place, was determined only recently. A couple of years ago a lady came into the pub and asked to look at the tiles; her son, she revealed, had made them as part of a commission for a house in the United States. Sadly the sale of the property fell though and the owner's grand plans came to naught and instead they ended up in Clerkenwell. In winter a real fire adds character to the front parlour and it is not unusual to see a party in the parlour periodically rotating, in the style of the Mad Hatter's tea party, in order to allow members of the company to warm up and cool off in turn.

The Jerusalem Tavern is notable for a number of reasons. It may not be authentic but something about it clearly resonates with Londoners. People all across London have heard of it, even if they have not been there and would not know how to find it, and it commands a respect and a following far beyond the office workers and growing band of Clerkenwell residents who make up its core trade.

For a small pub it can get very busy and will regularly turn over some 30 firkins a week – this is equivalent to seven and a half brewer's barrels or some 2,160 pints, which is going some. The beers come from the highly individual St Peter's Brewery, which is without doubt the best publicized firm of its size in the British brewing industry. At the tavern you can pick up a brochure which explains the origins of its distinctive medicine-bottle beers, the highly original recipes used in their extensive beer range, and their top-notch sister operations. Everything is performed with great attention to detail, a fact that Jerusalem regulars are not slow to appreciate.

Lamb Tavern

Leadenhall Market, City of London EC3V 1LR

BEERS: Young's Bitter, Young's Special, Charles Wells Bombadier, plus seasonal guest ales from London breweries

City traders working in the nearby Lloyd's building seek tradition and refreshment in the glorious surroundings of the Lamb Tavern

In some respects the Lamb Tavern is the best manifestation of what the City is about. Sited in the heart of historic Leadenhall Market on Bishopsgate, the City's main thoroughfare, the Lamb offers a glimpse of business as it has been done for centuries: that is, standing up. As you watch the City workers spill out of the doors of the Lamb to drink under the shelter of Sir Horace Jones's 1881 market you are witnessing a pattern of behaviour that has driven the City since Leadenhall Market was first established as a poultry market for 'foreigners' (non-Londoners) in the 14th century. They mill about, flit from group to group, meet old friends, make new introductions, shake hands on a deal, and move on. This is exactly how business was done in Sir Thomas Gresham's Royal Exchange (1567), the Stock Exchange (stock jobbing was first recognized as a trade in 1696) and Lloyd's of London (which originated in Edward Lloyd's coffee house in Tower Street in the 1680s).

The modern Lloyd's building designed by Lord Rogers is directly behind the market, and there is a public lift to an observation platform enabling you to look down inside Lloyd's impressive atrium to see the brokers scurrying about much as they do outside the Lamb. The pub dates back to 1780, though the present structure only goes back to the 1881 development, yet it is still a Grade II star listed building.

Leadenhall Market was sold to the City Corporation in 1411 and was declared a general market for poultry, victuals, grain, eggs, butter and cheese in 1445; wool and leather were added at a later date. The market was destroyed by the Great Fire and then rebuilt around three large courtyards – the first for beef; the second for meal, mutton and lamb (though fishmongers, poulterers and cheesemongers also had stalls); and the third yard was the herb market for fruit and vegetables.

The Morris family have run the Lamb for over 50 years, and will, therefore, remember its use as a film location in the John Wayne movie *Brannigan* (1975), the most notable of its film and television credits.

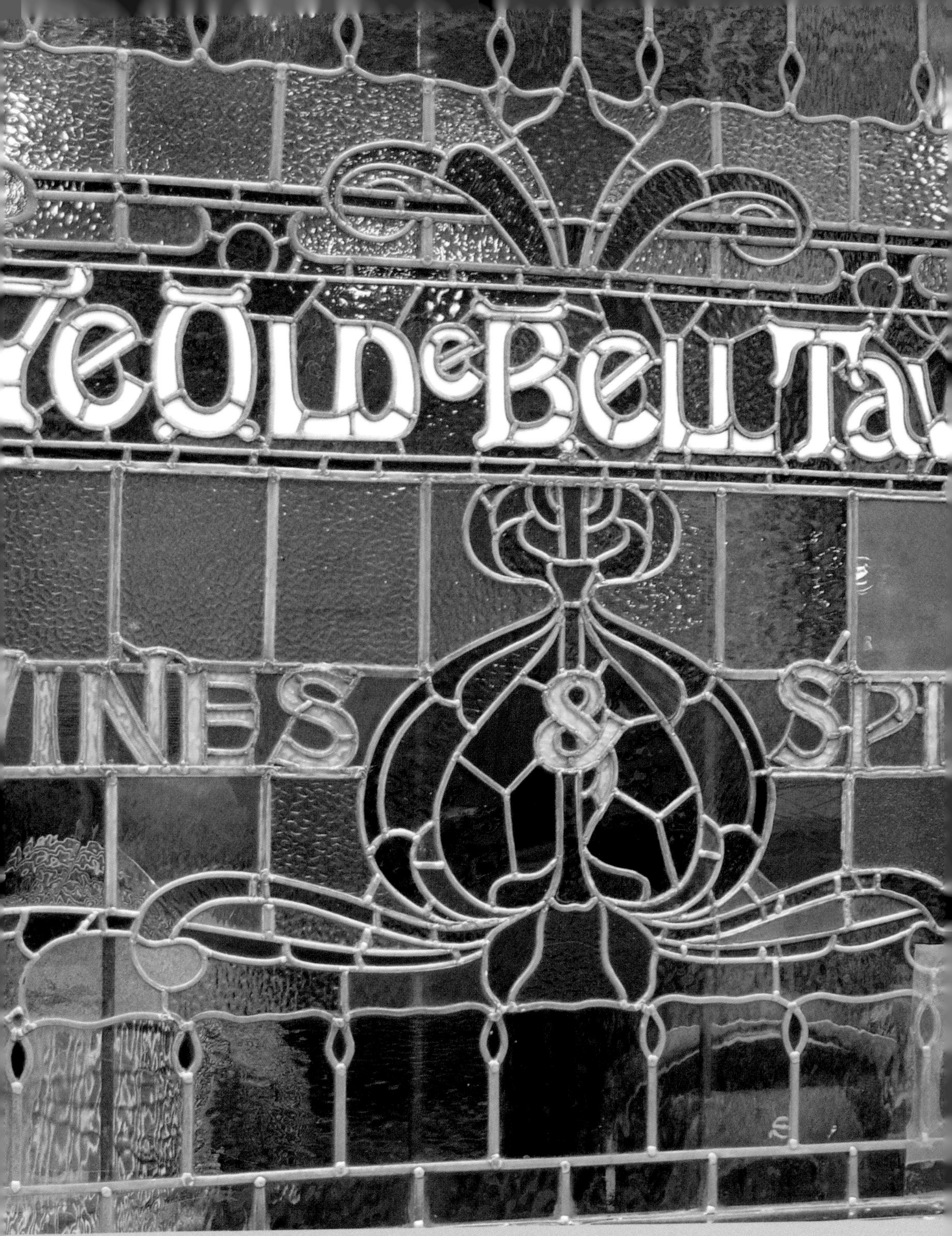
OLDE BELL
&

The Old Bell

95 Fleet Street, City of London EC4Y 1DH

BEERS: Sharp's Doom Bar, Tribute, Nicholson's Pale Ale

The Old Bell is an aristocrat among London pubs; traditionally a printers' drinking hole, it was designed by no less a figure than Sir Christopher Wren

Fleet Street's associations with printing and the press are well known, and it is hard to think of Fleet Street without thinking of the watering holes where generations of hacks have worked hard. None, however, has quite the ink-and-type pedigree of The Old Bell. A former tavern on the site, The Sun, was home to Wynkyn de Worde, former assistant to England's first printer William Caxton (c.1422–91), and de Worde's books were 'emprynted at the sygne of the Sun Flete Strete'.

The present building was designed by Sir Christopher Wren in 1670 as a hostel for workers rebuilding St Bride's Church after the Great Fire of 1666; architectural plans of the church adorn the walls. Unwittingly, Wren anticipated the practice of the 19th-century developers of the London suburbs who would build half a street starting with a pub, in order to claw back the wages of their labourers still engaged in the construction of the rest of the street.

Little is known of the tavern's history in the 18th century, but by 1833 it would seem that the premises were becoming respectable. Richard Etty, the licensee at that time, advertised that he 'continues his old system of cooking viz – Hot Joints daily from 12 to 7 o'clock; also mock turtle and other soups. Superior old wines, spirits, ale, stout etc. of the best quality and lowest terms.' By this time the Old Bell would have been just one among a number of taverns on Fleet Street, since the area was exempt from many of the public ordinances that applied west of Temple Bar (in the Strand) and east of Ludgate; that is, Fleet Street was free to offer all kinds of services not available elsewhere, and not all respectable either.

By the late 19th century the building was owned by the small Croydon brewery firm of Nalder and Collyer, who resisted the craze of the time for massive investment and refurbishment. This was because they expected The Old Bell to suffer the same fate as many great London inns and be demolished for road widening and sewer building. In the end, only a fraction of the building was lopped off, making it a valuable anthropological survival.

Old Red Lion

418 St John Street, Islington EC1V 4NJ

BEERS: Greene King Abbot Ale, Adnams Bitter, Adnams Broadside, Fuller's London Pride, Sharp's Doom Bar

The Old Red Lion, a comfortable pub with plenty of old-fashioned values, houses one of London's best-known fringe theatre spaces

A 10-minute walk from the King's Head theatre pub in Islington (see pp.140–141) is the Old Red Lion, a bigger pub, but a smaller venue. It is probably fair to say that the Old Red Lion is possibly the more adventurous and experimental of the two. It is also one of the City's liveliest pubs, both in terms of atmosphere and clientele, who are likely to be an arty and independent-minded bunch. This may have something to do with the proximity of City University, some 500 yards away.

The pub proudly proclaims itself to have been on the site since 1415, though the interior is rather more concerned with the here and now than with the styles of the early 15th century or even those of 1899, which is when it was rebuilt. Having said that, you will notice immediately that the pub is split down the middle by a 19th-century partition, and it is obvious that the pub followed the fashion of the day and was subdivided. The lateness of its re-building, after the bottom had fallen out of the London pub market, invites speculation, though, as to how the pub would have looked.

By no means all the evening clientele will be theatre visitors – locals, students, office workers, and the occasional soap star can also be found downing pints here – but if you particularly liked an actor's performance there is every chance that you will be able to buy a drink and discuss it with him or her after the show.

The pubs sign has been replaced and is no longer a lion rampant. Instead, a local artist has painted a picture of Rolo, the pub's friendly boxer dog.

The Palm Tree

127 Grove Road, London E3 5RP

BEERS: Two changing local cask ales always on

A surviving and still thriving East End pub in a much-changed landscape

If the Colton Arms (see p.160) is a slightly anachronistic survivor in West London then the Palm Tree is its East End counterpart. It too is a family-run pub whose personal nature has been key to its survival whilst the neighbourhood around it has changed out of all recognition.

There has been a pub on the site since at least 1850 and the present building was rebuilt by Truman's Brewery in 1929. Current tenants, ex-docker Alf Barrett and his more publican-minded wife Valerie, have been behind the bar since 1977, when the pub was at the corner of three adjoining streets.

Today the streets are gone: demolished in 1986 to make way for the Mile End Park. The Park was originally envisaged in the Greater London Plan of 1944, developed by Sir Leslie Patrick Abercrombie (1879–1957). It aimed to use the unique opportunity created by the destruction caused by the Blitz to put right the failing of the rapid and haphazard growth of the East End in the nineteenth century. Increased access for Londoners to green space was a big part of the Abercrombie Plan. Consequently the Palm Tree was also scheduled for demolition. It was only considered argument by Valerie in persuading the authorities that the pub could remain a viable local amenity that earned it a reprieve.

The Palm Tree has become something of an East End institution. True, the pub struggled during the redevelopment years, but clung on with the support of loyal regulars, some of whom have been visiting the place for 40 years. It's noted for

its décor – original postwar golf leaf wallpaper in the public bar – and its live music. The drums are left permanently in place. Above the bar are pictures of some of the many artists who have played there, although many of them will be more famous in the East End than nationally.

The Saloon is decorated on one wall with local Victorian photographs and on the other there are caricatures of several of the many professional boxers to have been produced by the East End; several caricatures were presented by the fighters themselves. The overall effect is to leave you in no doubt whatever about where in the world you happen to be.

The Palm Tree shares another feature with the Colton Arms. Here, too, they ring up your round into an old fashioned cash register. If you admire it, Alf will wryly inform you that it once fell into the canal – the Regent's Canal is only a few yards away – but it didn't sink. 'That's because it had a float in it'.

The Pride of Spitalfields

3 Heneage Street, Shoreditch E1 5LJ

BEERS: Fuller's London Pride, Fuller's ESB, plus guests

The Pride of Spitalfields has quite a country pub feel, and is a quiet oasis just a few steps from bustling, cosmopolitan Brick Lane

Kerry Butler, then landlord of The Pride of Spitalfields, died on 10 May 1996. On 8 August the staff of the Whitechapel Bell Foundry – the oldest industrial premises in the UK, founded in 1420 – paid him the impressive tribute of ringing a quarter peal of 1260 Plain Bob Minor on the six bells of Nicholas Hawksmoor's Christ Church Spitalfields. A quarter peal of Plain Bob Minor is a considerable amount of bell ringing, and not every publican who dies gets a peal of bells (though there is a strong argument that they should). Kerry Butler, we may deduce, was a much loved and much missed Spitalfields character.

The Pride of Spitalfields is a great little boozer tucked away off the increasingly colourful and trendy Brick Lane. It is an oasis of tranquillity and excellent beer – it serves a wide range of guest ales from Britain's 500-strong army of microbrewers. The pub is a great place to relax and soak up some local history.

It takes its name from the fact that the area was a centre of brick- and tile-making in the 16th century. The Truman Black Eagle Brewery established itself there in the 17th century, and by 1760 the Truman porter brewery was London's third largest brewery company; by 1873 it was the world's largest. Production ceased in 1982 when Truman, Hanbury and Buxton, still run by members of the founding families, became part of Watney's.

Brick Lane is best known as a symbol of successive waves of immigration, and young professionals seem to be the newest immigrants to flood the area. The first were Huguenots fleeing Catholic persecution in France. They settled in Spitalfields and brought silk weaving and textiles to the area. In the 19th century, Jews fleeing European pogroms were the newcomers (hence the 'beigel' shops at the north end of Brick Lane).

The strength of the Jewish community was demonstrated in one of the great events in London's history – the Battle of Cable Street. On Sunday, 5 October 1936 the local populace rioted when Oswald Mosley's British Union of Fascists planned to march through the East End. Mosley was humiliated, but the following week every Jewish shop in the Mile End Road had its windows smashed in London's own Kristalnacht. As the Jewish community grew affluent and moved out to north London the Bengalis moved in, and today Brick Lane, south of the brewery, is east London's curry quarter, and The Pride of Spitalfields is right in the middle. Today, the area is the focus of a trendy artistic community, which supports an ever-expanding array of design offices, coffee shops and restaurants.

A group of tour guides called Eating London regularly visit the pub, as well as a high number of Japanese tourists, as the pub cat is quite famous thanks to the Internet. The cat is called Lenny and has its own Twitter account: twitter.com/lennythepubcat.

The Punch Tavern

99 Fleet Street, City of London EC4Y 1DE

BEERS: Portobello Star, Sharp's Doom Bar, Revisionist Craft Lager, plus more than fifty varieties of gin

A superb interior, faithfully restored to its original Victorian style; outside, a gilded Mr Punch attracts the eye

A few doors away from The Old Bell stands another important Fleet Street pub, the Punch Tavern. Before the days of Rupert Murdoch, when printing presses made up Fleet Street, the Punch was synonymous with printers and newspapers.

Originally called the Crown and Sugarloaf, it became popular with the staff of the once great satirical magazine Punch, which was conceived there in 1841. Punch folded in the 1990s, to be rescued by the Harrods proprietor Mohammed Al Fayed. His largesse, however, was not endless and the title folded for a second time in May 2002, so proving the truth of the old joke about Punch which, supposedly, first started circulating in 1842: 'Punch. It's not as funny as it used to be.'

When the pub passed into new ownership in the 1890s it was renamed and refurbished in honour of the magazine. By another twist of fate, today's owners are called Punch Taverns, one of the country's new superpub companies, and they refurbished the pub once more. As it was just over a hundred years since the last fit-out, the place probably needed it.

On the whole they did a fairly good and faithful job, with the 1890s feel still much in evidence, along with countless examples of Punch humour from the Victorian and Edwardian eras.

It is a great pub interior, starting with the extravagant glazed and tiled lobby, continuing through to the ornate plasterwork, etched glass and huge bevelled mirrors of the saloon and finishing with Art Deco lighting – a mishmash of styles admittedly, but attractive nonetheless.

There is no doubt, however, that the pub has never fully recovered from the departure of the newspapers to the East End and beyond. Indeed, it used to be even larger, being a joint ownership between the two brewing giants, Bass and Sam Smith's of Keighley, Yorkshire. However, a falling out between the two companies only a few years ago resulted in the right-hand (Sam Smith's) side of the pub being abruptly bricked up; the bar actually continues through the wall into a now derelict room. It can only be hoped that the bars will one day be reunited.

The Royal Oak

73 Columbia Road, Bethnal Green E2 7RG

BEERS: Adnams Bitter, Timothy Taylor Landlord

Situated in the heart of London's most famous flower market, at Columbia Road, The Royal Oak does its best trade on Sunday mornings

If you walk down Columbia Road on a sunny afternoon you will quickly note that it is unlike the surrounding East End. For a start the south side of the street is a constant row of shops, but they are unlikely to be open. The street has a genteel feel and the shops carry arty, crafty names, and you will rapidly discern a theme – vases and pots, which mean flowers. If you are walking down Columbia Road on a sunny afternoon you have, in fact, made a mistake, for the time to go – when everyone goes – is Sunday morning. For Sunday morning is when the famous Columbia Road Flower Market takes place. Right at the heart of the market is The Royal Oak.

The flower market is a successor to Columbia Market, which was the idea of the philanthropist Baroness Burdett-Coutts, who wanted to wean costermongers off the streets. When it opened in 1869 Columbia Market was a quadrangle surrounded by elaborate market buildings, including a galleried mock Gothic hall and a clock tower which chimed a hymn tune every quarter hour. Needless to say, the costermongers preferred the streets, which is why Columbia Market no longer exists but Columbia Road Flower Market does. The pub opens at 8am on a Sunday to offer breakfast to the market traders and customers, many of whom have been busy buying and selling well before that. As with most London markets, the professionals arrive early and as the morning wears on the public turn up in increasing numbers.

Columbia Road is a place nearly every Londoner has been to at least once. Unlike other London street markets – Portobello Road, for example – which get crowded with casual tourists, the fact that the flower market takes place when most Londoners are still in bed means it is always busy but never overcrowded, and the fact that everyone is there to buy and not just to browse gives it a special buzz. If you do go, linger – as the morning drags on bargains appear.

Not far from Columbia Road is Brick Lane, once home to the Truman Brewery. Not surprisingly, many East End pubs were Truman houses (Charringtons in the Mile End Road was the other big East End brewer, while Whitbread was in the City in Chiswell Street), and equally unsurprisingly breweries tended to develop a house style in their pub refurbishments (they often had their own architectural departments). The Royal Oak is very much a Truman house. Lots of wood panelling, the distinctive Truman type face and the frosted windows all shout Trumans. Visit The Gun in Brushfield Street and count the similar features, or look at The Birdcage at the other end of Columbia Road for another example of a Truman style with its bottle green tiles.

A bit sleepy when the market is not on, vibrant and bustling when it is, The Royal Oak and the flower market are true living London and living links with the London of times past.

The Three Kings

7 Clerkenwell Close, Clerkenwell EC1R 0DY

BEERS: Timothy Taylor Landlord, Harvey's Sussex Best, Woodforde's Wherry

The eclectic and unusual pub signage represents the many artisan groups that practise in Clerkenwell

You should not be misled into thinking that in order to be included in this volume pubs have to be historic or picturesque. Eccentric and welcoming will do just as well, and when it comes to these characteristics The Three Kings has them in spades. The pub is fairly traditional on the outside with two windows advertising it as a former Mann, Crossman & Paulin house – a firm that disappeared into the Watney's maw in 1958, proving that this pub has longevity indeed by London standards.

One of the reasons why The Three Kings survived is, perhaps, that for many years Clerkenwell was a not a very fashionable area. Despite being one of

the oldest quarters of London – the Fons Clericorum or Clerks Wells which gave the area its name date back to the 12th century and were situated where the parish church of St James is now, across the road from the pub – the area was overlooked and neglected. The Karl Marx Memorial Library made its home here in 1933: Lenin had worked in this old Welsh Dissenters School when in exile in 1902.

As is frequently the case with run-down areas, the people who spotted its potential were artists and artisans, a fair share of whom have clearly had a hand in shaping the style and appearance of The Three Kings. A carved rhinoceros head hangs over the mantelpiece, and various ornaments are made out of papier-mâché, including the inn sign, which depicts three kings – King Henry VIII, King Kong and Elvis the King. Each letter of the pub's name represents a different craft or trade to be found in the locality, although engraving does not seem to be represented – despite the fact Clerkenwell is a local centre of engravers, servicing major customers in Hatton Garden's jewellery stores.

The local clientele are a definite change from the suited types to be found in the City pubs further south. Clerkenwell Visitors Centre sits across the street from the pub, next door to the Church of St James, where martyrs of the Reformation are remembered. To the north are the remains of the House of Detention, one of London's early prisons, which is worth a visit though it remains largely unknown to most Londoners; and just a few yards to the south is Clerkenwell Green, dominated by the old Middlesex Sessions House.

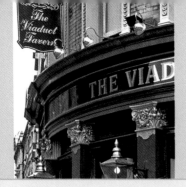

The Viaduct Tavern

126 Newgate Street, Holborn EC1A 7AA

BEERS: Fuller's London Pride, Fuller's ESB

This large pub has a Victorian interior that cannot fail to impress

Very popular with postal workers from the Giltspur Street depot, The Viaduct is notable for having one of the most striking Victorian pub interiors in the whole of London. The ceiling is ornate lincrusta – a form of lightweight covering made of pressed paper and linseed oil. On the east wall are three remarkable representations of 'Agriculture', 'Banking' and 'Arts'. Sadly, Miss Arts was attacked and shot at by a drunken soldier celebrating the end of the First World War, and she still bears the wound today.

Further back there are some fine mid-Victorian mirrors which are just right for the period of the pub, which was built in 1869 and named after Holborn Viaduct. The viaduct itself, which is also replete with female allegorical figures, was opened by Queen Victoria in the same year as the pub. It is likely that the pub was built in the knowledge that much of the cost would be recouped from the viaduct's construction workers and navvies.

The pub boasts a rare and handsomely carved cashier's office, a legacy of the early days of the gin palace style and hints at what the pub's original windows may have looked like. A clue to the possible fate of these may be gleaned from the wall of the watch house in Giltspur Street attached to the Church of the Holy Sepulchre, which bears the legend 'built 1791, destroyed 1941, rebuilt 1962'.

The cellars were originally the cells of Newgate Prison which was directly across the road, and the bar staff will happily show them to customers. The pub also boasts not one, but two ghosts: one called Fred, who lives in one of the cells, but has been known to come up to the bar, and the ghost of a prostitute who was murdered here and who enjoys turning off the toilet lights. Famous past patrons include Oscar Wilde who visited during his trial at the Old Bailey, and though you are unlikely to get anything quite as scandalous as his famous case you are well advised to cross the road to the Old Bailey itself, ring on the bell and ask for admittance to the public gallery, for a Central Criminal Court trial can rank among the best free theatre to be had in London. Purchased by Fullers in 2006, this Grade II-listed building has lost its bar surround.

Ye Olde Cheshire Cheese

145 Fleet Street, City of London EC4A 2BU

BEERS: Sam Smith's Old Brewery Bitter

As its sign purports, and fine but rickety wood-panelled interior confirms, this pub really is 'olde' – the current building dates back to 1667 when the pub was rebuilt after the Great Fire of London

Ye Olde Cheshire Cheese is a historic London pub that is certainly well worth a visit. This warren of rooms dates from shortly after the Great Fire of London of 1666, when the pub was rebuilt. The site is much older and covers the cellars of the Bishop of Peterborough.

Famous for its associations with Dr Samuel Johnson, the lexicographer, wit and celebrated 18th-century man of letters, the pub remains very much as Johnson would have remembered it. The main bar is splendidly dark, sporting a sawdust floor and a real fire next to which Charles Dickens used to like to sit, beneath the 1829 portrait of a former waiter, William Simpson. To the left of the Gentlemen's Bar is the Chop Room, a traditional-style London 'ordinary' with booths formed by high-backed settles, providing privacy and grandeur. On upper floors are other dining rooms, some available for private hire, including the famous Johnson Room. To the rear the Cheese is divided into secluded areas and quiet snugs, with a modern extension behind to cope with the pub's popularity.

The establishment seems to have had several golden eras. In Johnson's day his drinking friends included portraitist Sir Joshua Reynolds, Edward Gibbon of The Decline and Fall of the Roman Empire and David Garrick, the actor/manager. A century later came Thomas Carlyle; Alfred, Lord Tennyson; Charles Dickens; John Forster, biographer, historian and journalist; W. M. Thackeray; George Cruikshank, the caricaturist and illustrator; and Wilkie Collins. Later still came Mark Twain, Theodore Roosevelt, Sir Arthur Conan Doyle, G. K. Chesterton, Max Beerbohm and W. B. Yeats. In many ways the true heyday of the pub was the 1920s rather than the 1770s, for it was then regarded as Fleet Street's finest.

For many years the pub owned a foul-mouthed parrot, Polly. On Armistice Day 1918 it imitated the sound of champagne corks popping some 400 times before fainting. When it died in 1926 obituaries were reported in some 200 newspapers around the world, including the North China Star.

A great Cheese tradition that has sadly been lost was their Christmas pudding. Of mammoth dimensions, each year it included a portion of the previous year's pudding, making it continuously the world's oldest dish.

Ye Olde Mitre Tavern

Ely Place, Holborn EC1N 6SJ

BEERS: Fuller's range, Caledonian Deuchars IPA plus regular guests

The hard-to-find Mitre Tavern is worth seeking out; once there, enjoy a drink while reading up on the establishment's colourful history

By rights this pub should not be in this book – it is such an excellent establishment that people are initiated to the Mitre by swearing never to disclose its location. Being one of the best hidden pubs, however, there is a good chance that even with directions you may never find it and the author will never have to undergo the blood-curdling forfeit that is inflicted on those who break the oath of secrecy. Another, more solid, reason why the Mitre should not be in this book is because, technically, it is part of the demesne of the Bishop of Ely, and until a few years ago its liquor licence was granted by magistrates in Cambridgeshire rather than London.

The solid chairs in the back bar are from the Bishop's Palace that used to stand nearby. Ely Place became the town residence of the bishops of Ely during the early 14th century, and the first pub was built in 1546 by Bishop Goodrich for palace servants. Indeed, in the front bar is a post carved from a cherry tree (which Queen Elizabeth is reputed to have used as a maypole) that marked the boundary of the bishop's garden and the land 'leased' to Sir Christopher Hatton. In fact, Hatton effectively commandeered the land and paid the bishop the lordly rent of one red rose a year.

The Mitre is full of history, and it is advisable to ask for the printed history which details the full story of the pub, the bishops of Ely and Sir Christopher Hatton, as well as that of the nearby church; the latter, dedicated to St Etheldreda, the 7th-century founder and first abbess of the monastery at Ely, is also well worth a visit.

Nestling behind the famous Hatton Garden jewellery stores, Ye Olde Mitre has been the refuge of many a beau in need of a stiff drink after realizing the extent of the damage inflicted on his wallet. From the upstairs bar it is possible to peer into the windows of jewellers' workshops, where craftsmen create and repair jewellery for Hatton Garden, making this and neighbouring Clerkenwell among the few remaining artisanal quarters in London.

The present pub dates from 1772 and is very much an alehouse in the traditional sense, trading on its excellently kept ales. Space precludes culinary activities any more ambitious than a toasted sandwich, but you will be surprised at how many sandwiches they can turn out. The author is clearly not the only one who can't keep a secret.

MARYLEBONE TO BELGRAVIA

This area is the home of the mews pub, born through the aristocracy's desire to keep their staff happy and quiet and the town planners' desire to keep vulgar pubs hidden away. These alehouses have survived the 20th century's changes in society and class structure and now cater for a more wealthy crowd than stablehands and domestic servants – although stablehands from the Hyde Park Riding School still enjoy a drink in this part of town.

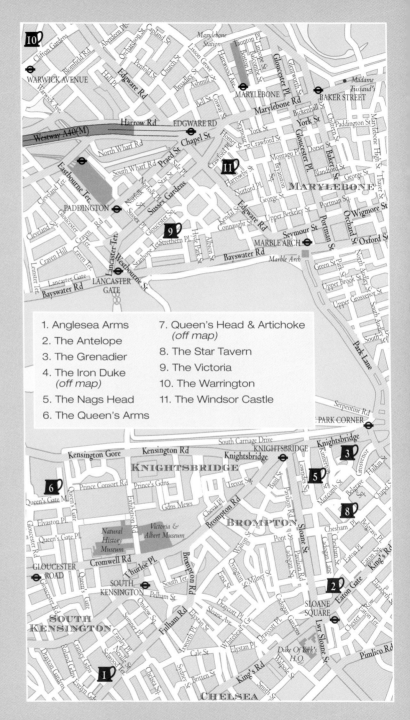

1. Anglesea Arms
2. The Antelope
3. The Grenadier
4. The Iron Duke
   (off map)
5. The Nags Head
6. The Queen's Arms
7. Queen's Head & Artichoke
   (off map)
8. The Star Tavern
9. The Victoria
10. The Warrington
11. The Windsor Castle

Anglesea Arms

15 Selwood Terrace, South Kensington SW7 3QG

BEERS: Adnams Bitter and Broadside, Young's Bitter, plus guests

The Anglesea Arms is a handsome pub with a fine pedigree suited to its locality – although it started out as a pub serving market gardeners

Built around 1825, the Anglesea Arms lies on the site of a market garden and nursery, which dates back to 1712 and was once owned by a Mr Selwood. In the early 18th century this part of Kensington was a village with several market gardens, all busy supplying a hungry and expanding London. Appropriately, the road on which the pub sits was named Salad Lane, before becoming Swan Lane and then Selwood Terrace. The road shares literary connections other than William Cobbett, the famous journalist and social commentator, who was a colleague of Mr Selwood. The young Charles Dickens stayed at 11 Selwood Terrace in 1835 and his fiancée Catherine lived round the corner in York Place. Also, D. H. Lawrence lodged at No. 9.

Today, the pub is a genteel, open-plan modern treatment of the Victorian theme. Original features give it its charm, while bare floors and plain wood tables are very much à la mode. To the rear is a dining room, with wood-panelled walls and high-backed chairs, giving it a rather Hanoverian air, and offering a wider menu.

Clues to the tastes of the clientele can be gleaned from the presence of a selection of Havana cigars for sale and the wine vintage chart on the pub table cards. Beyond wine, however, the pub has had a reputation for good beers since the 1970s, when it was one of the first free houses to sell real ale from independent brewers.

Major attractions in the area include fine eateries on the Old Brompton Road and excellent shopping on the Fulham and King's Roads; further north are the Royal Albert Hall, the Kensington museums and Kensington Gardens.

The Antelope

22 Eaton Terrace, Belgravia SW1W 8EZ

BEERS: Fuller's London Pride, Fuller's ESB, plus guests

The large island bar defines The Antelope and makes conversation with your neighbours, whether you know them or not, very much the done thing – hence the convivial atmosphere

The Antelope could only be in SW1. It has a feel about it. You could not pick it up and put it down anywhere else without it looking like a fish out of water. Since it is in just the right place it feels comfortable, and a pub that feels comfortable is a pub that has got it right.

Built as a mews pub, albeit on a corner site, in 1827, when Belgravia was being transformed from an area of notoriety into one of gentility by Thomas Cubitt's major redevelopments, it was intended to cater for a mews clientele: servants, footmen, ostlers and the like, and its essentially spartan character bears witness to this. Its charm is its unaffectedness. It is a place where you come to stand at the bar, gossip and laugh. Those who would like to eat can be catered for at lunchtime,

though the old dining room, famously divided into booths, is no longer in operation.

The Antelope is very much a locals' pub, after its own fashion, and whereas pubs in east or south London might have a prize draw, or a meat raffle, or a pool league to act as a point of common interest, The Antelope has a cricket club: the walls are decorated with team photos and the club roll of honour.

The pub itself is fairly small, with a large island bar. A small, snug-like room to the left compensates for any overcrowding at busy times, and to the rear are old-fashioned settle-type seats of the kind that were once the hallmark of the alehouse, but which are all too rare today. The Antelope is wonderfully unspoilt.

The Grenadier

Old Barrack Yard, Wilton Row, Belgravia SW1X 7NR

BEERS: Adnams Bitter, Adnams Broadside, Fuller's London Pride, Greene King IPA

Famous for its Bloody Marys and at least one bloody death, hence its reputation for being haunted by the ghost of a card-cheat officer

The Grenadier is one of that select band of pubs that people deliberately seek out as destinations in their own right. In this case the particular attraction is the Bloody Mary for which the pub is internationally famous. On a Sunday lunchtime there is even a special Bloody Mary bar, behind which a usually overworked barman turns out a constant supply of the spicy cocktails as fast as he can shake them. On their best ever Sunday they managed to serve some 300 – that's some shaking.

Tucked away behind Wilton Crescent off Belgrave Square, the pub was originally the Duke of Wellington's officers mess, and outside in Old Barrack Yard are the remains of the duke's mounting block and stables. The pub was then known as The Guardsman and was popular with King George IV. In later years it became The Grenadier and is still popular with officers of that regiment when they are on ceremonial duties at the nearby royal palaces.

The pub itself is quite small and adorned with guards mementoes and memorabilia. The pewter bar is original, extremely rare and may be the oldest of its kind. A narrow ledge runs around the bar area for people to rest their drinks on; there is very little seating. To the rear is a restaurant which specializes in traditional English fare. On sunny days most customers will spill out into Wilton Row to enjoy their drinks, which are frequently accompanied by another speciality of the pub, a sausage on a stick served with a dollop of ketchup and a dollop of mustard.

Britain boasts many haunted pubs, but London remarkably few, maybe because your average ghost is no match for your average Cockney. The Grenadier is an exception, and is reported to be haunted each September by a guards officer who died when overenthusiastically flogged for cheating at cards. The Grenadier is an ideal spot to perk yourself up after a visit to the Duke of Wellington's residence, Apsley House at Hyde Park Corner.

The Iron Duke

11 Avery Row, Mayfair W1K 4AN

BEERS: Fuller's Discovery, London Pride ESB, plus seasonal beers

Excellent Fuller's pub named after the first Duke of Wellington and full of interesting mementoes

Here cheek-by-jowl, some of the world's richest people sit with ordinary folk and enjoy a luxurious pint of one of Fuller's fine ales. The West London brewer certainly knows how to run a good pub and The Iron Duke, in the heart of glamorous and well-healed Mayfair, is no exception.

The area was first developed between the mid-17th and 18th centuries as a fashionable residential district, taking its name from a 15-day May Fayre which was once held there. The Iron Duke is a short walk from Grosvenor Square, the home of the US Embassy and a famed statue of Franklin D Roosevelt. The narrow and appealing Avery Row, is one London's many almost-secret passageways, providing a short but interesting walk from Grosvenor Street, passing jewellers, fashionable

tailors and antique shops, before crossing Brook Street and joining South Molton Street.

Over the years the pub has known many incarnations. It was once a Yates Wine Lodge but today it is a smart, comfortable pub and a welcome find in an area where some pubs promise much but deliver little. Named after Arthur Wellesley, the 1st Duke of Wellington who, in 1815 with the help of Prussian forces under von Blucher, defeated Napoleon at the Battle of Waterloo. He was given his nickname, the Iron Duke, not for his military prowess but for his opposition to parliamentary reform. In 1829 he was forced to erect iron shutters at Apsley House, his London home, to prevent it from being broken into by angry crowds.

This Iron Duke is far more inviting; outside, large colourful flower baskets frequently decorate the smart exterior and, though there are no outside tables or seated area, customers will often stand in the street to observe office workers and shoppers passing by. Inside the neat, tasteful, L-shaped bar is decorated with many mementoes of one of Britain's most distinguished military commanders and politicians. One tells the story of the Wellington Boot (the Duke is credited with its creation); it was the height of fashion in 1815, when it was supposed to be ideal for battle yet still comfortable enough for a gentleman to wear in the evening.

The menu is simple and a good antidote to the area's many gastro pubs – the pie is particularly recommended. Like all true pubs, you can sit with a beer in the Iron Duke and later decide to eat without any pressure to order an expensive meal.

Nags Head

53 Kinnerton Street, Westminster SW1X 8ED

BEERS: Adnams Bitter, Adnams Regatta, Adnams Broadside

The Nags Head is famous for having the lowest bar top in London; this highly unusual feature is due to the sunken serving area and is accommodated by tiny bar stools

'The upstairs bar was designed about a hundred years ago to encompass the frame of one working man at a time. Today this same bar is forced to accommodate 40 or 50 gentlemen, often with the effect that one of them may be expelled into the street with the velocity of an orange pip angrily fired from between the thumb and forefinger of an ill-disposed gorilla.' So wrote

one rather excitable fan of this truly great pub in 1963, when it could still uphold its claim to being the smallest pub in London. If an ill-disposed gorilla did choose to frequent The Nags Head it is unlikely that it would raise much comment. The locals are an eccentric enough bunch themselves and tend to take folk pretty much as they find them.

Built in 1775, Kinnerton Street was a row of stables, and the tavern may have been added in the 1820s. The walls of the Nags Head are a mass of in-jokes, caricatures and cartoons of regulars, including former local, the actor James Mason. There is a small, fine collection of antique amusement machines of Allwins and the end-of-the-pier variety, while a shelf at picture-rail level is crammed with pub clutter of the finest quality.

The pub is most unusual in that the bar service area is lower than the floor, meaning that the staff are looking up at you, and the bar counter itself must be one of the lowest in Britain. Pride of place on the bar belongs to a fine antique beer engine, which still sees service dispensing three Adnams ales.

At the rear is a larger room, down a short flight of stairs, but the locals tend to prefer the top bar, and it is the locals who really make this pub, and will happily drag you into a conversation.

With real fires adding to the cheery glow, the Nags Head is a delightful place to while away an hour or two, all to soundtracks from the 1930s and 1940s. The best time to visit is on a Sunday when the locals have the place to themselves and Kinnerton Street seems to forget that it's in London; there's also live jazz on the first Sunday of each month.

The Queens Arms

30 Queen's Gate Mews, Kensington SW7 5QL

BEERS: Fuller's London Pride, Sharp's Doom Bar, Timothy Taylor Landlord, plus 5 guests

Like many of London's best pubs, The Queens Arms is tucked away, so true pub lovers will make a point of seeking it out

Considering how much there is to do and see in South Kensington it is remarkable how few pubs there are in the neighbourhood, and of those how few are even half decent. The best, by far, is The Queens Arms, tucked away in Queen's Gate Mews. Perhaps it is this out-of-the-way location that has saved it, but certainly you need to know it is there as a chance encounter is unlikely.

This mews pubs was intended, as readers who have encountered other mews taverns will by now know, to serve the countless servants of the wealthy families who lived in 19th-century Kensington. Little by way of original features remain in this large one-bar boozer.

The Royal Albert Hall is just three minutes' walk away. Queen Victoria laid the foundation stone on the site of the former Grove House on 20 November 1868 and she returned to declare the building open on 29 March 1871. In the years since, countless millions have followed in her footsteps in order to see the big-name acts of the day.

The Queens Arms is the place to go after a concert, but do not dawdle on leaving the hall as the pub fills up extremely fast making it difficult to get served. When you do get served, though, you'll have plenty of choices, with a total of eight ales on tap, rare for a pub of this size (which variously offers from 23 different beers).

Queen's Head & Artichoke

30-32 Albany Street, Regent's Park NW1 4EA

BEERS: Whitstable Brewery, East India Pale Ale, Sharp's Cornish Coaster, Mahou

Sympathetically restored Victorian pub a stone's throw from Regent's Park with an excellent reputation for food and a cosy atmosphere

The Queen's Head & Artichoke is a snugly bustling pub at the bottom of Albany Street. One of London's best pubs for foodies, it serves excellent modern English cooking alongside a lengthy tapas menu. Food is served in the cosy downstairs bar or in the smartly comfortable first floor dining room, which is also available for private hire. The excellent Sunday brunches and roasts confirm this pub's place in the very upper end of so-called 'gastro pubs', a term that is so often shorthand for a lacklustre pub experience.

Dating from the 16th Century, the Queen's Head and Artichoke was once a royal hunting lodge. It appeared in Crew's Survey of 1753 as a ramshackle old tavern. When Regent's Park was built, several well-known inns were demolished one of which, the Queen's Head and Artichoke, was moved to Albany Street. It was rebuilt on the present site in 1811, though the existing building dates from around 1900.

The licence itself dates from Queen Elizabeth I. The origin of its name is attributed to one Daniel Clarke, master cook to both Elizabeth I and James I, and Queen Bess's head gardener who ran the place.

The Queen's Head and Artichoke is well worth dropping into if you are looking for refreshment in this part of town. The Cumberland Gate of Regent's Park is a short walk away, and if you have time, wander a little further to see Regency architect John Nash's magnificent Cumberland Terrace with its grand portico of Ionic columns. A drink in the Queen's Head and Artichoke would be an ideal prelude to a performance in the famous open-air theatre in Regent's Park.

The Star Tavern

6 Belgrave Mews West, Belgravia SW1X 8HT

BEERS: Fuller's London Pride, Fuller's ESB, Fuller's Seasonal Ale, Gale's Seafarers, Oliver's Island Golden Ale, plus guest

The Star Tavern, one of Fuller's Brewery's top houses, has a strong local following but also attracts visitors from far and wide

It is easy to imagine liveried footmen and jodhpured stable lads taking their ease before the real fire in The Star Tavern, as it has something of the tack room about it. It is almost certain that such characters would have been customers when this handsome Georgian mews pub was built.

One can be in little doubt that this is a Fuller's house since mirrors, signs and plaques shout the brand at you everywhere you look. The right side of the pub consists of the bar, where the regulars congregate, and the other side opens out to a long, broad, airy room divided in two by a gentle arch. Both sides are warmed by a rare solid-fuel fireplace. On the first floor is a dining room which has the distinct feel of a gentleman's library.

The pub does remarkably good business even at weekends, given that it is not in a hugely residential area, being located to the rear of Belgrave Square, the heart of London's diplomatic quarter. Indeed, it is very much a destination pub, and is doubtless commonly recommended by the doormen and concierges of the Knightsbridge hotels, judging by the number of foreign visitors who manage to find it. Actually, there is no shortage of first-rate recommendations in this neighbourhood, for also tucked behind Belgrave Square one can find The Nags Head (see p.108) and The Grenadier (see pp.104–105).

Belgrave Square takes its name from a Leicester village and was laid out in 1826 when the Earl of Grosvenor obtained an Act of Parliament allowing him to build there. Developed by Thomas Cubitt, it was the design of a pupil of the great London architect Sir John Soane, George Basevi, cousin to the future prime minister Benjamin Disraeli. Damp clay was dug from the ground and made into bricks on the site, and the workings were filled in with soil from the excavation of St Katharine's Dock (see Dickens Inn, p.72).

Nearby attractions include Buckingham Palace, Hyde Park and Apsley House, all of which are only five minutes' walk from The Star.

The Victoria

10a Strathearn Place, Bayswater W2 2NH

BEERS: Fuller's Chiswick Bitter, Fuller's London Pride, Fuller's ESB

A stunning example of high-Victorian style, the Victoria is not without its own royal pretensions, and the long-lived 19th-century monarch and her family are celebrated all over the walls

If you emerge from either Lancaster Gate or Marble Arch tube stations and enter the triangle of land bordered by the Bayswater Road, Sussex Gardens and the Edgware Road, you will find yourself in Tyburnia, so named to rival Fitzrovia at the other end of Oxford Street. It takes its name from the Tyburn gallows which were originally sited near Bond Street tube, where Stratford Place meets Oxford Street. As the city expanded the gallows gradually moved west and ended up at Tyburn Tree, where Edgware Road meets Marble Arch. Speakers' Corner in Hyde Park owes its origins as a place of free speech to the proximity of Tyburn, for the simple reason that if you were about to execute someone in public there were precious few sanctions left at your disposal to prevent them from saying what happened to be on their mind.

Just round the corner from Westbourne Street is The Victoria, a pub with a truly magnificent interior. This luxurious Victorian tavern, with its sumptuously ornate mirrors and a carved bar back, achieved some fame in the 1960s when a painting on the wall was discovered to be a valuable portrait of a member of the royal family; it is now part of the Royal Portrait Collection. Today, royal portraits are not in short supply at the Victoria – Queen Victoria, her consort and her children appear over the fireplace at the west end of the pub, balancing the large mirror at the other end of the room. The size of the room and the contrasting style of its two fireplaces suggest that it may once have been split into two.

There are many items of interest to be found at this establishment. In the bar there are superb

mirrors that continue the royal theme with their fleur-de-lys pattern, and hunt out the unusual tiles that can be found above the wall-hung prints. Don't miss the upstairs 'Library', a delightful place for a private function, and the 'Theatre Bar', complete with lots of theatrical memorabilia and having very much the feel of a West End theatre bar.

The Warrington

93 Warrington Crescent, Maida Vale W9 1EH

BEERS: Fuller's London Pride, Young's Bitter, Shepherd Neame Spitfire, plus guests

The Warrington was acquired by celebrity chef Gordon Ramsay in 2007, resulting in some changes to the décor, mostly sympathetic

An impressive frontage greets those turning into the broad sweep of Warrington Crescent: pillars of Babylonian intricacy form the main approach to the pub. Step over the Romanesque mosaic bearing the pub's name and enter a rich and unique interior. Not all is authentic in this Edwardian hostelry, but the later additions are either sufficiently well executed or sufficiently tongue in cheek to get away with it. Note in particular the Aubrey Beardsley-esque mock Art Nouveau nudes that adorn the carved awning over the beautifully complex bar: in a faux-marquetry style, they turn out to have been painted by Colin Beswick in 1965 and work exceptionally well.

Satisfyingly dark woods interact with dark reds in the carpets and William Morris-style wallpaper on the ceiling to give the correct patina to the pub.

The darkness is broken up by mirrors, which in turn are divided by carved wooden mouldings, and doors and screens with stained glass that combines Art Nouveau with more classical designs.

Facing the bar, marble pillars support intricately carved wooden arches, which guide the eye to the heavily balustraded staircase leading up to the Thai restaurant on the first floor, one of the first of several Thai restaurants to have made a home in London pubs.

Built in 1859 and remodelled in the 1990s, the pub was originally a hotel, albeit one with a dubious reputation – it was allegedly a brothel, which must have caused some consternation to its owners, the Church of England. The pub was also a famous haunt of jockeys and members of the racing fraternity, one of whom once won £100 by riding a horse up the steps and into the pub.

The Windsor Castle

27–29 Crawford Place, Marylebone W1H 4LJ

BEERS: Young's Special plus guest ale

National pride exudes from The Windsor Castle, and although some may find the hectic interior overwhelming, it is undeniably engrossing

The Windsor Castle is one of the great hidden pubs of London. Although it is just off the busy Edgware Road it is unknown to all but a few who pass that way. This is a pub just as people would like to imagine pubs to be, beautifully eccentric and a total confection of all the landlord's whims and fancies. If the locals like it too, then all the better. In this case the landlord's fancies clearly include the British royal family. Seemingly every commemorative mug and plate produced for a royal event over the last 70 years is on display here. Entire walls are devoted to royal family prints.

Above head height are a number of signed prints of film stars and celebrities who have been as charmed by The Windsor Castle as you will be. The windows are stuffed with eclectic collections: coloured sands, porcelain bottle stoppers and glass ashtrays with a royal theme; Toby jugs crowd the shelves; there are vintage bottled beers, cameos, and even the tables double up as a history lesson.

Not surprisingly, this is a pub that attracts devotees. The names of many of them, past and present, are engraved on brass plates screwed to the bar. The Handlebar Club meets here on the first Friday of the month. This is, of course, the club for gentlemen sporting stupendous handlebar moustaches, some of which are several feet in length.

This is a superbly English pub – once inside you are spirited away to a land of deference and good manners. However, incongruously with the rest of its character, the pub does serve good Thai food.

The Windsor Castle is the kind of pub that just grows better the more you learn about it, and it certainly bears repeat visits. When the locals are in you might even start to believe that there is good in the world, and all cynicism starts to dissipate.

NORTH LONDON

It being in the nature of Man to divide into nations, nations to divide into tribes and tribes into clans, it is not surprising that within a fiercely proud city such as London there is a strong rivalry between north and south Londoners. Northerners deride the south for its lack of tube lines, while southerners point to

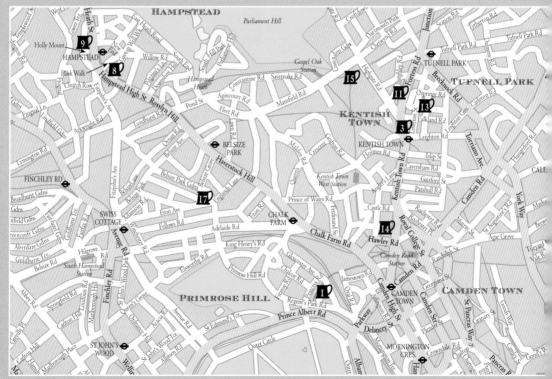

north London's absence of decent pubs. Although much of north London is a publess urban sprawl, there are still plenty in its leafy villages, such as Highgate and Hampstead, and some of these are among the best the metropolis has to offer. Whether you choose The Albion in Islington or head slightly further afield to Hampstead's famous (and infamous) Spaniards Inn, you won't be disappointed.

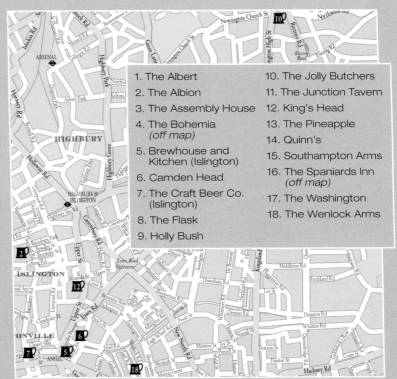

1. The Albert
2. The Albion
3. The Assembly House
4. The Bohemia (off map)
5. Brewhouse and Kitchen (Islington)
6. Camden Head
7. The Craft Beer Co. (Islington)
8. The Flask
9. Holly Bush
10. The Jolly Butchers
11. The Junction Tavern
12. King's Head
13. The Pineapple
14. Quinn's
15. Southampton Arms
16. The Spaniards Inn (off map)
17. The Washington
18. The Wenlock Arms

The Albert

11 Princess Road, Primrose Hill NW1 8JR

BEERS: Greene King IPA and Abbot, plus guest

The Albert is a great place to get modern British food in a traditional English atmosphere

The Albert is a medium-size Victorian pub which has received the modern treatment in a most sympathetic and successful fashion. Bare wood floors and a motley crew of non-matching wooden tables and chairs in different styles are in vogue, as are the fresh flowers on each table. The history is confined to the walls and ceiling, and very handsome they are too. To the rear is an airy conservatory, leading to a secluded garden which takes a spreading apple tree as its focal point.

Food is very much the business of the pub, which specializes in modern British cooking at pub prices. Built in the 1860s, the pub was named after the then recently deceased consort of Queen Victoria. Albert was a hugely popular figure, and his considerable energies and dynamism as a modernizer and proactive champion of innovation were both recognized and appreciated. A glimpse of this may be seen on the walls, where a number of informatively annotated Albert-related prints demonstrate the measure of the man.

The Albert's lovely garden is a great place to soak up the sun, but if you decide you want some more space then Regent's Park is nearby. The pub is also suitably located for enjoying many other north London attractions: the bargain-shopping delights of Camden Market; Primrose Hill is a local beauty spot; and London Zoo – a good full-day attraction which should leave you with an appetite that the Albert can do justice to.

The Albion

10 Thornhill Road, Islington N1 1HW

BEERS: Greene King IPA, plus Guest

A wonderful place for a relaxing drink, either in the cosy, mismatching armchairs inside or the attractive garden at the back

There are still cobblestones in the little village-like corner of Islington in which the Albion lives. It is a handsome Regency-style inn, although little of this is visible beneath the thatch of vegetation – ivy, wisteria, hanging baskets and window boxes – that covers the whole. Unsurprisingly, the pub has won quite a few London in Bloom awards.

Inside there has been an impressive programme of restoration and modernization, even if it is now more of a gastro pub than a local. It was recently voted one of the top 50 places in the country for Sunday lunch by a national newspaper.

French windows in the restaurant lead through to a marvellous wisteria-filled garden and with its regular barbecues this is the perfect place for a meal outside in the sunshine.

The style of the building suggests it was a coaching inn, as is depicted on the inn sign, though you should take care to spot the sign's deliberate mistake. It is, however, doubtful that it ever was a coaching inn, due to the fact that it has never been on a coaching route – although the main route to Liverpool did pass quite close by.

The Albion is a popular place, and well known in the Islington and Barnsbury area as a handy alternative to the constantly busy pubs of Upper Street. Catch the Albion when it's not too busy and it is a wonderful place for a relaxing drink.

The Assembly House

292-4 Kentish Town Road, Kentish Town NW5 2TG

BEERS: Morlands Old Speckled Hen, Greene King IPA, Ruddles County

Londoners tend to forget that their public houses often provide some of the finest architectural features in the city; it is often worth standing back from the building to absorb it as a whole

The Assembly House takes its name from a building of 1796 that was a meeting point for people gathering together to make up a party before setting off for Hampstead Heath and other places north – the occasionally vain hope was that travelling in numbers would deter the highwaymen who infested the woods and lanes along the roads at this time (see The Spaniards Inn, p.148).

This beautiful late Victorian pub, has, like thousands of others, reinvented itself to perform

under modern conditions and appeal to the modern eye. As is often the case, the ceiling provides the best clues as to how this massive space was formerly arranged. A little inside knowledge always helps, too. The area under the glass dome – note the mid-Victorian glass at odds with that elsewhere – was originally a billiard room; on the other side of the chimneypiece was the dining room; what is now the narrowest part of the bar was once a private members' room; and the area that is now set lower than the rest was a public bar. All in all, it forms a very fine example of late Victorian pub architecture.

A particularly striking feature of The Assembly House is its considerable size. Such Victorian pubs needed large spaces to accommodate the large number of activities that went on in them as well as the large number of staff employed.

Original features have been retained, yet the pastel walls, easy chairs, settees and a lighter use of contemporary materials, prints and colours in the front bar give the place that feeling of ease that both translates the pub's historic function into the modern day and makes for a friendly space. This latter consideration has had a huge influence on the appearance of pubs (country inns excluded): now that women constitute over 50 per cent of the workforce it is a commercial necessity to appeal to them. Pubs you cannot see into from outside are a dwindling proportion of the total pub stock, yet within living memory they were all like that. The Assembly House is a good example of how the feel of even a grand old Victorian gin palace can be softened up.

The Bohemia

762–764 High Road, London N12 9QH

BEERS: Own house beers, plus wide range of guest ales and bottles

*One of London's best operators shows what can be done
and why the suburbs are where it's at*

Dan Fox cut his operational teeth at the pub trade finishing school that is the White Horse, Parsons Green (see p.189), before taking over the Bull, Highgate, putting it on the map as a fine ale and fine food pub with its own in-house brewery. Opened in June 2014, the Bohemia is his London Brewing Company's second venture. This former O'Neills had been taken over and renamed by the previous owners before they went into administration; Dan rescued it, refurbished it and realised it had sufficient space to make it London's largest brewpub in terms of production capacity. Located at the rear of this long narrow building is a fairly chunky piece of brew kit. A 6.5 barrel (10 hectolitre) brewhouse sits in a well recess, whilst out back are no fewer than six 13 barrel (20 Hl) fermenters and maturation vessels.

American diner style décor set amid plenty of space gives it bags of character with which to welcome the largely local clientele, around 1,000 of whom signed a petition to Save the Bohemia when it was in difficulty. It is to these people that Dan is paying most attention. Accessibility is his watchword. Yes, there are 25 draught beers on at any time, including around eight of his own, but these are not aimed solely at the hipster aficionado. Dan says, 'Being local comes before being a destination. We want to be a great pub before being a great beer pub. As 80% of our customers walk here, we want them to feel comfortable rather than try to sell them the world's most obscure beer'.

If you do want to embark on the journey of beer discovery, there are well-informed staff to assist. At least once a month the brewing takes place in the evening so customers can see – and smell – the process up close. There are also monthly launches of their new seasonal beers, whilst the food offering focuses on fresh seasonal British pub food with an emphasis on cooking with beer and beer matching.

A recurring theme in this edition of the book is the extent to which London's vibrant and thriving beer and pub scene is in the midst of a golden age, but the surprise is how the exciting and innovative stuff is happening in the most unexpected places. It's not the centre of town, it's not necessarily even trendy Hackney and Dalston; North Finchley's where it's at. Get away!

Brewhouse and Kitchen

5 Torrens Street, London EC1V 1NQ

BEERS: A selection of ales brewed on the premises, plus A-list international brands

A superior brewpub, setting the beer right at the heart of the show

There are, at time of writing, nine Brewhouse and Kitchens. At time of reading, there may well be more. The two that live in London are at either end of Upper St. The younger is the old Tram Shed (which was an old tram shed) at Highbury Corner and which contains the group's largest brewery (five and half barrels). The elder is tucked behind Angel tube and contains the group's smallest brewery.

Simon Bunn and his business partner Kris Gumbrill both had many years' experience as operators in the pub trade and had been friends for 20 years before Simon saw a brewhouse concept in Ostend and thought it would translate well to the UK.

That was in 2011. 2012 was spent raising capital, defining the concept and looking for suitable sites. The first, in Portsmouth, opened in March 2013. Having proved the idea they have gained momentum and further sites have been added in Poole, Bournemouth (two), Gloucester, Dorchester, Bristol, and now two in London.

What marks the concept out is the simplicity of the plan. There's a clue in the name. Décor is a big part of the mix of any pub, but few brewpubs manage to successfully incorporate the brewery into the look and feel of the place. Too often they are hidden, or incongruous, or an added-in extra. Not here. As soon as you walk in, your eye is drawn to the beautiful copper lustre of the carefully lit brewhouse, which then informs the design of the bar area and remainder of the layout, in a way that is welcoming and inviting rather than cold and industrial.

Each Brewhouse has its own brewer, who, provided they aren't just fixated on making 8% ales, is given free range to design their own beers, the names of which take their inspiration from the immediate locality. The emphasis is very much on pairing quality beer with quality food and on laying to rest the popular myth that wine is a better companion to food than beer. It isn't. Engaging the customer is also a big part of what the brewers are expected to do. For £99 you can have a day with the brewer, work alongside him, get fed and watered and even return later to carry off some of the fruits of your labour. If Islington isn't part of your regular stamping ground, worry not. At this rate there will almost certainly be a Brewhouse and Kitchen coming soon to a neighbourhood near you.

Camden Head

Camden Passage, Islington N1 8DY

BEERS: Courage Best, Courage Directors, Charles Wells Bombardier

At the Camden Head the public house meets the music hall in harmonious symphony; the pub is a wonderfully authentic period gem

Upper Street, the start of the Great North Road, is a long, straight mile of little else but restaurants and pubs. Just off Upper Street, however, it is a different story, Camden Passage is a little enclave of antique and curiosity shops.

The Camden Head is a magnificently preserved Victorian gin palace with more than its fair share of interesting features. There is a rare pair of water taps on the bar enabling customers to add just the right-size drop of the only thing you are allowed to add to malt whisky apart from more malt whisky. There is a pair of gin globes, sadly incomplete, but exceptionally rare none the less, and there are fine tiles, mirrors and an impressive back bar, or stillion.

There is also a theme: casual perusal will reveal a connection with music hall. A few yards away on Islington Green, in what is now a branch of Waterstone's bookshop, once stood the Collins Music Hall, which functioned from 1862 to 1958, making it London's last operating music hall. The building was gutted in 1963. The connection between this music hall and the Camden Head was clearly symbiotic. Indeed, as the Camden Head is home to one of London's many pub comedy clubs, which are merely music halls in modern garb and which seem to have multiplied consistently in the last decade, the wheel might be said to have come full circle.

The Camden Head allows one to enjoy the best of what Islington has to offer without having to contend with the scrum of Upper Street. The Screen on the Green, one of London's most intimate cinemas, is nearby; the Regent's Canal is reached by ambling down Duncan Street; the Business Design Centre is one of the powerhouses that contribute to Islington's trendy dynamism, in sharp contrast to the traditional outdoor London life of nearby Chapel Market. For those seeking theatrical pleasures, the King's Head Theatre (see pp.140–141) is only a stone's throw away, and Sadler's Wells is just two stones' throws.

The Craft Beer Co.

55 White Lion Street, London, N1 9PP

BEERS: A wide range of changing cask beers, keg beers, ciders and bottled beers

A welcoming North London alehouse that shows what can happen when all the elements fall into place

When Martin Hayes and his partners opened the Cask and Kitchen in Pimlico in 2009, he probably never imagined that he was just about to catch the wave that has been the London craft beer revolution. Martin went on to found the Craft Beer Company in 2011 to, in his own words, 'be the finest establishment in the UK for good beer on cask, keg or bottle'.

Today they have six pubs (including in Brighton, Clerkenwell, Clapham, Brixton and Covent Garden), which together boast 127 keg taps and sell 104 cask ales. They are fine establishments all, but it is the one in Islington that wins out by having that intangible je ne sais quoi that makes a great pub out from a good pub. So what is this elusive magical element?

The previous owners clearly didn't have it. In its last incarnation the Lord Wolseley was the kind

of microwaved food boozer that was increasingly struggling to find a place in a changing world. The recession killed it off. However, recession also created many opportunities for London's pubs and exponentially expanding fraternity of microbrewers, and landlords faced with empty or failing properties were grateful for the arrival of the likes of Martin, who came equipped with a vision.

That vision can be heartwarmingly simple too, as it is here. It is simply to offer good quality, uncomplicated food and beer in a welcoming environment where you can 'snuggle up somewhere', maybe; when you drop in there will be someone playing the piano in the corner – that old cliché about the old London knees up Mother Brown rub-a-dub that is actually rarer than moon dust. Here locals come to support the local bands who play, and non-locals are drawn by imaginative events like the Vintage Ales Festival or the Smoked Beer Festival which are put on periodically, but not so often they annoy the regulars.

Simple visions still require an eye for detail which means having good staff who understand and share the vision; you don't need to spend very long here to see that this is the case. You will be greeted by someone knowledgeable who is as eager to take you on a journey into beer as they are to simply pour you a drink, and who believes that there is a beer or cider that is right for everyone and whose job it is to help you find it, or, if it's what you want, is happy to just leave you alone so you can get on with the serious business of 'snuggling up somewhere'.

The Flask

14 Flask Walk, Hampstead NW3 1HE

BEERS: Young's Bitter, Young's Special, plus 3 guests

The Flask is a genteel place to drop in to for refreshment after a hike around Hampstead Heath; choose between the public or the saloon bar

The Flask owes its name to a philanthropic bequest of 1689 when 'six acres of waste land lying and being about certain medicinal waters called the wells' were given over to the benefit of the poor of Hampstead. The wells being the only positive feature of the land, the trustees of the bequest hit on the idea in 1700 of bottling the water

and selling it to the public at three pence a flask. The margins on bottled water in the 18th century being every bit as huge as they are in the 21st, the waters were carted to the Thatched House, as the pub was then called, bottled and despatched throughout London to quench the thirst and ease the pains of the upper classes. This was the century of the spa towns such as Bath and Tunbridge Wells, so not surprisingly Hampstead became fashionable – and has remained so ever since.

Remarkably, The Flask remained thatched until 1874, when the building was replaced. Today, the pub is divided into four distinct areas. The front saloon contains the original features, including five painted panels dating from the 1880s, which are unusual in that they follow no particular theme. To the rear is a rather more contemporary drinking area, opening up to a conservatory added in 1990 and decorated with prints of old Hampstead. At the front is a simpler public bar, separated from the saloon by the same screen that supports the painted panels. In the public bar these panels are filled with tasteful prints of old Hampstead.

Lino floors and no frills mark out The Flask as one of the dwindling number of pubs that maintain a definite difference between the public and saloon bars. At one time this would have been underlined by the fact that beer bought in the public bar would have been a penny or two cheaper.

The pleasures of Hampstead Heath are only a short walk away, and there are further pubs for you to enjoy as you go.

Holly Bush

22 Holly Mount, Hampstead NW3 6SG

BEERS: Fuller's London Pride, Adnams Ghost Ship, plus guests

Most London pub fans have at least heard of, if not visited, Hampstead's Holly Bush, which until recently was still gas-lit

The Holly Bush is one of London's most famous pubs, and many Londoners are likely to have been there at some time or other. Dating back to 1643, the pub was made famous by its association with local residents. The painter George Romney lived and worked next door, and what is now the rear of the pub was formerly his stables, which were incorporated into the pub on his death in 1802. Romney's house was converted into the Hampstead Assembly Rooms, to which the Holly Bush acted as caterer. The pub was, therefore, familiar to an even more famous Hampstead resident, John Constable, who is known to have lectured at the Assembly Rooms in 1836.

The Holly Bush was, however, no stranger to illustrious visitors before Romney and Constable, as James Boswell and Samuel Johnson, Oliver Goldsmith, Leigh Hunt and Charles Lamb are all known to have drunk there. In later years it gained popularity with the stars of music hall; Marie Lloyd was a patron, and, Hampstead being the neighbourhood it is, celebrities from the literary and television worlds can still be seen there on occasion.

The pub has undergone various changes throughout its history. It was one of the last London pubs still to have gas lighting, and it replaced them only recently. This has altered the character of the front room somewhat, although the fire in the grate is still real. A new snug has been created where the gentlemen's toilets once stood, and to the right of the bar is possibly the smallest snug in any pub anywhere.

The Jolly Butchers

4 Stoke Newington High Street, Stoke Newington N16 7HU

BEERS: Wide range of beers from UK craft brewers and the wider world

Stoke Newington's ale and cider house with a good selection of unusual beers and robust, modern pub grub

If imitation is the sincerest form of flattery then the Southampton Arms in Kentish Town (see p.146) should be very flattered indeed. It has become a bit of a talking point that the Jolly Butchers, which took on its current guise in 2010 has a similar 'Ale and Cider House' sign to the Southampton, set up some months earlier. But then people like to talk in Stoke Newington, it is that type of place. The locals at the Jolly Butchers, many of whom work in the media and public relations, have raised chattering to a new level of expertise.

And where better to talk than at one of the many wooden tables of different vintages and styles, looking like they have been saved from ending up in a junkyard, which now populate the Jolly Butchers.

This is a must-visit pub for many of the area's beer lovers who until recently had to travel to other parts of London in search of good and unusual beers. Indeed, if you are a lover of good beers and ciders, conversation and robust modern style pub grub there are few better places.

Stoke Newington is an eclectic place, full of independent-minded people drawn from the four corners of the world. It always seems to have been that way and that sense of freedom and diversity is reflected in the Butchers' beer list. The pub, which is situated just a couple of minutes walk from Stoke Newington railway station and just around the corner from the sometimes twee Church Street has a range of speciality beers not just from the UK but from around the world.

It includes German weissbeers, Belgian kriek and Vedett on tap. Many of the beers come from London's new brewers including the Camden Brewery's excellent Camden Stout. Also on tap are Brew Dog products. Brew Dog is a recently established Scottish brewer which has taken the beer world by the scruff of the neck and given it a good shaking. The brewer, like its beer Zeitgeist and the excellent Jolly Butchers, has captured the 'spirit of the times'.

The Junction Tavern

101 Fortess Road, Kentish Town NW5 1AG

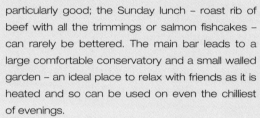

BEERS: Caledonian Deuchars IPA, plus wide range of guests

Excellent Sunday lunches and a great variety of guest ales, many from independent regional breweries, make this pub an extremely pleasant place to while away some time

This is just the place for a long, lazy Sunday afternoon, so don't be put off by the dark exterior. The Junction Tavern, a classic Victorian pub a few moments' walk from Tufnell Park and Kentish Town stations, must have worn many different masks over the years but its latest minimalist incarnation has not damaged its lovely period features which include some extravagant wood panelling at the rear.

The front of the bar area is dominated by a large, open kitchen where chefs work fervently to produce food of the highest quality and the Junction is rightly renowned for its menu. The food is modern, made from locally sourced ingredients wherever possible. The fish and chips are

particularly good; the Sunday lunch – roast rib of beef with all the trimmings or salmon fishcakes – can rarely be bettered. The main bar leads to a large comfortable conservatory and a small walled garden – an ideal place to relax with friends as it is heated and so can be used on even the chilliest of evenings.

Background music is often playing – and the rhythms of the world make this a very traditional London pub. This area of London is a place of constant flux; many of the Junction's cosmopolitan customers seem to be aspirant models, musicians or media stars, talking over their dreams across pints of beer. The founder of communism Karl Marx once lived in the area and, who knows, perhaps he sat in the Junction with a beer, united with some of the workers of the world, discussing class struggle and the collapse of industrial capitalism.

Currently the pub is CAMRA's (Campaign for Real Ale) North London Pub of the Year with five cask ale pumps on the bar. Each week it offers around fifteen different guest ales from regional breweries and, in addition, regular beer festivals are held when more than 40 ales are on sale. Recently featured beers include Cornish Mutiny from Wooden Hand Brewery in Cornwall, and the award-winning Pieces of Eight from Nelson's Brewery in Chatham, Kent. The pub's management try to offer the very best from independent regional breweries, but also feature what they consider to be the best of the big boys. The house ale, Deuchar's IPA, is a light, hoppy, golden ale from the Caledonian Brewery in Edinburgh.

King's Head

115 Upper Street, Islington N1 1QN

BEERS: Young's Ales, Camden Town Beers, local craft breweries in bottle and on tap

Eccentric and theatrical – in every sense of the word – the King's Head takes on the various roles of pub, restaurant and front of house

Not so much a pub as a theatre with a great front of house. The King's Head has been a pub theatre since 1969, before which the auditorium was a boxing ring. It is probably the most famous of London's numerous pub theatres, the largest concentration of which lies in and around Islington (such as the Hen and Chickens and the Old Red Lion, see pp.82–83), as it is one of London's slickest fringe venues and attracts very good productions, many of which go on to greater and more lucrative things.

The theatre motif is unmistakable from the moment you set eyes on the pub, with walls covered with framed shots from former productions featuring many familiar actors who started out here before hitting the big time. The door to the theatre space also stamps its presence, giving the pub something of the feel of a stalls bar from one of the older West End theatres.

There is also a programme of live music every night Thursday to Sunday, though this tends, obviously, to take place after a theatre performance has ended since the auditorium is just to the rear of the pub. If you prefer your pints after a production, you can attend an evening show or a weekend matinee.

The Pineapple

51 Leverton Street, Kentish Town NW5 2NX

BEERS: Doom Bar plus guests

Pubs can arouse passion – thankfully, as it was the people who felt passionately about the Pineapple who saved this great local pub

Just round the corner from the Assembly House (see pp.124–125) lies a more modest but much-loved local boozer of great character, The Pineapple.

The Pineapple, which reopened on 18 May 2002 after refurbishment, is successfully fulfilling a traditional function in a contemporary style. A function room at the rear, sensitively done, in no way detracts from the charm and exuberance of this fabulous place.

The pub was originally built in 1868, and is now a Grade II listed building as a consequence of its many unusual pineapple motifs and because of a vocal local campaign to 'save The Pineapple', after the widow of a former occupant sold the property to developers for conversion into flats.

Pineapple regulars and local celebrities, such as actors Rufus Sewell and Ken Stott, newscaster Jon Snow and even London Mayor Ken Livingstone became involved in the campaign. Listing the building scuppered the developers' plans and it was sold on to the current owners, who want to keep this handsome and wonderful backstreet pub open to supply the goods, services and functions that the Pineapple and countless pubs like it have traditionally provided.

It is hard to put a price on the importance of a pub to its local community. There is really no such thing as a traditional pub. Pubs are traditional because, oft times past, people have habitually used them and continue to do so. It is not the pub that is traditional, it is what it does and what people want from it that is.

In London the vast majority of pubs date from the 1890s, whatever the date of the fabric of the building.

The term 'pub' did not come into usage until the mid-19th century and was then used to describe improved business premises selling beer that were attempting to distinguish themselves from the gin palaces of the 1820s and 1830s. Prior to this most retail outlets for beer were alehouses, which were very basic affairs, often little more than the front parlour of a private dwelling. The term 'public house', which arose from the recognition that alehouses were primarily private dwellings, did not come into popular usage until most alehouses had been transformed into primarily commercial premises.

Princess of Wales

22 Chalcott Road, Chalk Farm NW1 8LL

BEERS: London Pride, Adnams Bitter, Wadworth Malt & Hops, plus guests

Dedication to its long-standing locals, well-kept beer and a friendly, welcoming atmosphere mark this pub out from the crowd

The 'village' of Primrose Hill is tucked behind Regent's Park and London Zoo, a collection of wide, tree-lined streets and elegant houses. The hill and sloping park around it cover 112 acres; one of the highest points in London, at 206 ft, it boasts wonderful panoramic views across the city once you have puffed your way to the top.

The area has a colourful history: the medieval seer Mother Shipton predicted that if London ever grew big enough to surround it, the streets of the city would run with blood; later, during the reign of Henry VIII, it formed a hunting forest together with Regents Park. In the early 1840s, the land was bought by the Crown from the Eton Estate and made into a public park by an Act of Parliament. The name of the area is said to come from the primroses that bloomed here in the 17th century. Blue plaques in the neat, stucco-fronted roads commemorate past residents of note, including the poets Sylvia Plath and W.B. Yeats.

The Princess of Wales has stayed mercifully clear of the sort of refurbishment that tends to affect gentrified parts of London and this is something to be truly thankful for. This is a warm, genuine pub, featuring large windows (which fold back on warm days) and cosy nooks for romantic winter days.

Although this is not really a foodie pub, there is a good choice of reasonably priced pub grub, as well as excellent Sunday lunches. The pavement seating, is complemented by a beer garden at the rear of the pub and an airy conservatory .

The live jazz on Sunday evenings, the Tuesday quiz night and the warm welcome for dogs contribute towards making this place a proper pub for locals, attracting regulars of all ages – a refreshing change from other 'destination'-style pubs in the area. If style over substance is your thing, this isn't the pub for you, but if you are looking for a good, honest, friendly boozer with well-kept ales, the Princess of Wales is highly recommended.

Quinn's

65 Kentish Town Road, Camden NW1 8NY

BEERS: Green King Abbot Ale plus 3 guests

Quinn's is a colourful, family-run pub, and a fantastic example of what a pub can be when run with a light heart and a dedication to brewing

A fine example of a modern treatment of an older interior, which works because it has been done with attention to detail by people who care. Quinn's is an Irish pub of the best kind. London is full of Irish pubs, most of which owe no more connection to Ireland than they do to Antarctica. 'Plastic Paddy' pubs are easily recognizable because they scream a faux Irishness at you. They are also conspicuous because Irish people studiously avoid them. Quinn's is Irish because the Quinns – who have run the pub with their three sons for 15 years – are Irish, and they bring their love of the trade to the bar.

The pub dates from the early 1800s, though under the Quinns' stewardship it doubled in floor space in 1991 and was further altered in 2001. The centrepiece of the pub is the 15-metre long bar and beautifully carved and illuminated back bar. On the opposite wall the windows are painted with a crude but fun series of tableaux of Edwardian dining-room and drawing-room scenes. These, combined with a sprinkling of various Art Nouveau devices, lends the place a slightly Belgian feel. As luck would have it, Quinn's does a fine range of Belgian beers, as well as a selection of bottled beers from Germany and France – the list runs to around 70; there is a considerable draught range too, more than enough to satisfy the most persnickety connoisseur. This means that Quinn's has a much wider than average range of beers on offer.

Quinn's is just outside the main catchment area of Camden Market but is well worth the short extra walk, and it is near enough to the Regent's Canal to access all the delights that lie on its banks.

Southampton Arms

139 Highgate Road, Kentish Town NW5 2RF

BEERS: An ever-changing range of beers, cider and perry from some of the country's best independent producers

London's self styled ale and cider house might look old but it is one of a new wave of pubs putting the heart back into their local communities

The secret of the Southampton Arms is simplicity itself. Take a tired, run-down boozer, throw out the forlorn carpets, strip the wooden floor and decoration back to the basics, add in some former church pews and wooden tables and a wood burning fire that pierces the chill even on the coldest day, sell an ever-changing range of 10 draft beers and eight ciders and perrys from Britain's independent craft producers and give customers the chance to choose what comes next. And don't bother with an extensive food menu and the tantrums of a temperamental chef, just serve proper pork pies, real Scotch eggs, handmade sausage rolls and keep a joint of pork with crackling for putting into baps.

In under 12 months Peter Holt has transformed a pub which most people quickly walked by on their way down towards Kentish Town or up towards Gospel Oak into a must-visit pub for anyone who cares about what they sup and is passionate about the provenance of our national drink.

Sometimes it can get very crowded, with the crush relieved just a little as people spill out into the small beer garden-patio at the back. On other occasions it is the perfect place to sit and relax with a newspaper, chat with friends, or even just watch the world go by through the large windows which overlook the constant bustle of Highgate Road.

Most beers are served in smart dimpled glasses with a handle – which seem to have been shunned by lager drinkers and fans of keg beer for a generation. And what a choice of beers there are including Magic Rock, Marble, Howling Hops and Tiny Rebel. A range of cider and perry is always available, something which was recognised by the Campaign for Real Ale when the consumer organisation named it the best cider pub in London. Ciders from producers Burrow Hill, Oliver's and Severn Cider are regulars among its six cider handpumps. Not many pubs sell a perry (the alcoholic drink made from pears), but the Southampton Arms distinguishes itself by selling two.

The background music comes from a vinyl-playing turntable behind the bar and a piano at the end of the bar is not for show. A pianist often plays on Wednesdays and Sundays. This is a real pub which deserves its success.

The Spaniards Inn

Spaniards Road, Hampstead NW3 7JJ

BEERS: Sharp's Doom Bar, Fuller's London Pride, plus 3 guests

Take the stories that surround The Spaniards Inn with a pinch of salt; truth need not always crowd out romance, though, and The Spaniards is undoubtedly a very romantic pub

The Spaniards Inn is one of London's most famous pubs, and this means that it is very much on the tourist trail but still very much worth a visit. As much remains unknown about the pub as is known. There are about as many theories as to the origin of the name as there are authorities on the subject. Some say it is named after a Spanish ambassador to James I's court, who used it as a refuge from a summer plague ravaging London. Others claim that it was named after a Spanish landlord named Francisco Perrero. Yet even more believe that it took its name from two Spanish brothers who once ran it. There are even those who maintain that these two brothers once fought a duel over a lady, which led to the demise of one.

Dick Turpin the highwayman was certainly associated with the pub, though do take what you hear of him with a large pinch of salt. He is said to have been born in The Spaniards, but there is equally strong evidence to suggest that he was born in The Crown in Hempstead, Essex. Certainly Essex was very much his patch (see The Black Lion, p.70), and much of the Turpin legend is just that – legend. What *is* known about him is that he was a viscious lout who certainly never deserved any kind of posthumous celebrity, and his famous ride to York almost certainly never took place in the fashion related. Ironically, when arrested in York in 1739, he was using the alias John Palmer, which was the name of the Bath theatre manager who went on in 1784 to found the Royal Mail coaches specifically to contend with the likes of Turpin.

At The Spaniards you will also hear of its role in foiling the Gordon Rioters intent upon destroying the house (now Kenwood House) of Lord Mansfield in 1780. Mansfield had infuriated the anti-Catholic mob and it was only the action of the landlord in throwing open the Spaniards' cellars, so causing the rioters to forget the task in hand for long enough for the militia to arrive, that prevented the destruction of the mansion.

It remains, therefore, only to say that the list of wits and wordsmiths familiar with The Spaniards is very long. Charles Dickens famously used it as the location for Mrs Bardell's tea party in *The Pickwick Papers*, and Bram Stoker also used it in the darker work *Dracula*.

The Washington

50 Englands Lane, Belsize Park NW3 4UE

BEERS: Sharp's Doom Bar, Adnams Broadside, plus 3 guests

A rich abundance of high-Victorian craftsmanship sets the Washington apart from its neighbours in Primrose Hill

A modern, food-oriented pub set in Victorian surroundings, The Washington must surely be unsurpassed – in North London certainly – in terms of the sheer number of original fittings.

Walking up Primrose Hill Road one is met by George Washington winking at you with an enigmatic smile. The plainness of the inn sign and frontage disguises the feast of finery that hits you when you enter. So sit down at any of the rough tables provided (one is even an old butcher's block) or cosy up on a sofa and prepare to spend a goodly while taking in all the detail.

Look at the varying styles running through the glass panels, mirrors and wood panelling. Are there two eras represented here, or even three? You should admire the mirrors at the rear of the pub on the left side, both astonishingly rare survivals of mid-Victorian high taste, and exceptionally well preserved ones at that (see The Alma, pp.172–173,

for comparison), with exquisitely painted birds and wild flowers in enamel.

Observe the shape of the bar counter, which blends in beautifully with the moulded wood panelling, and see if you can guess where the missing partition would have been that once divided the pub into three. One partition, or part thereof, remains, and creates a more intimate and secluded area to the rear, popular with those of the canoodling persuasion.

You can also admire the wood carving around the mirrors, which bears such classic legends as 'Champagnes of Noted Brands in Stock', or 'Old Ports and Sherries of the Choicest Vintages'.

There is much more to enjoy than is outlined here, and the pub's current stewards have managed to create a very pleasant modern ambience in the space without in any way detracting from what was there already.

The Wenlock Arms

26 Wenlock Road, City of London N1 7TA

BEERS: a constantly changing range of 10 cask ales, 15 keg beers, and 8 ciders from around the British Isles

Yet another notoriously difficult-to-find pub, but as the Wenlock Arms is one of London's finest alehouses persistence pays off

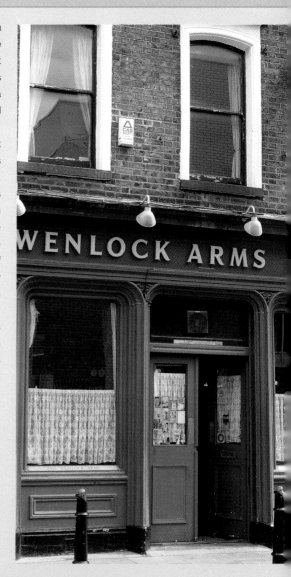

The Wenlock Arms is a destination pub in a quiet corner of London, just at the edge of the City but without sharing the City's wealth and just on the edge of Islington without sharing Islington's designer chic. A formerly forlorn locality, the area is mainly residential with some light industry and offices, and is opposite the Shepherdess Park.

It is unlikely that even in its heyday The Wenlock ever attained the fame that it enjoys today, for it is north London's premier real-ale house bar none. It serves a terrific range of regularly changing ales and at any one time an impressive number are on tap. The Wenlock is something of a champion. The clientele are a knowledgeable crowd, and will be only too happy to talk you through the full range of ales and beer styles on offer, including both new London craft brewers and the best brewers from around the British Isles.

Ale is not the pub's only attraction, however. It is also a music pub of repute. Sunday lunch-times is the slot for Holly Roberts, who can make a piano do just about anything short of sit up and beg. There is also live music some evenings; just check the pub's Twitter page (@wenlockarms) for the next event.

The pub, with its handsome central stillion, surrounded by an impressive array of highly eclectic beer bottles, features a large blackboard displaying not only the beers currently available, but, importantly for bringing customers back again, the beers that are currently acquiring condition in the cellar.

The Widow's Son

75 Devons Road, London E3 3PJ

BEERS: No real ales; national brands available

A typical East End pub with its own special tradition

The actual date of establishment of the Widow's Son pub is a bit of a mystery, as is just about everything associated with this East End legend. Most academic references give a date of around 1848 for the construction of the building, although the glass mirror inside the pub clearly says 'Est 1793'. What is not in doubt is that the pub was built on the site of a row of cottages, one of which was home to a widow whose son left to go to sea and never returned. Legend has it that he kissed his old mum goodbye with the injunction to keep a nice hot cross bun ready for him as he would be home for Easter. Each year she baked a new one and hung it up to await his return. Upon her death a net full of buns was found hanging up in her cottage.

Whether this be true or not, what is certain that the tale has given rise to one of the great traditions of East London, for, to this day, every year on Good Friday a number of sailors visit the pub and the youngest amongst them adds a specially baked new bun to those in the net over the bar.

A mysterious fire in the 1980's closed the pub for a while and destroyed a number of the buns, which explains why some of the older ones look rather charred. It also explains why the front (damaged) portion of the pub is rather plainer than the (undamaged) rear, which is home to one or two nice original features. The pub has a nautical feel with lots of sailors caps and badges adoring the walls as reminders of Good Fridays gone by, though what the Rat Pack – whose pictures adorn the wall opposite the bar by the pool table – would make of the tradition is anyone's guess.

The pub is Grade II listed and is undoubtedly an important part of the history of Bow, but it is under threat from developers. You can do your bit to help save the Widow's Son by going there yourself.

WEST LONDON

West London's pubs abound with wisteria and whimsy, but are also wonderfully diverse. Some are old country pubs that have seen a city grow up around them, while others, including The Tabard, were built as and when the surrounding streets emerged. There is a wealth of delights to uncover, be it as you meander along the River Thames in the footsteps of England's great designer and writer William Morris (1834–96) or as you pound the pavements along the King's Road in search of a place to quench your thirst after a hard day's shopping for the latest fashions.

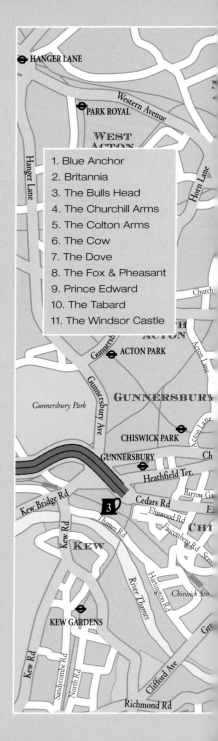

1. Blue Anchor
2. Britannia
3. The Bulls Head
4. The Churchill Arms
5. The Colton Arms
6. The Cow
7. The Dove
8. The Fox & Pheasant
9. Prince Edward
10. The Tabard
11. The Windsor Castle

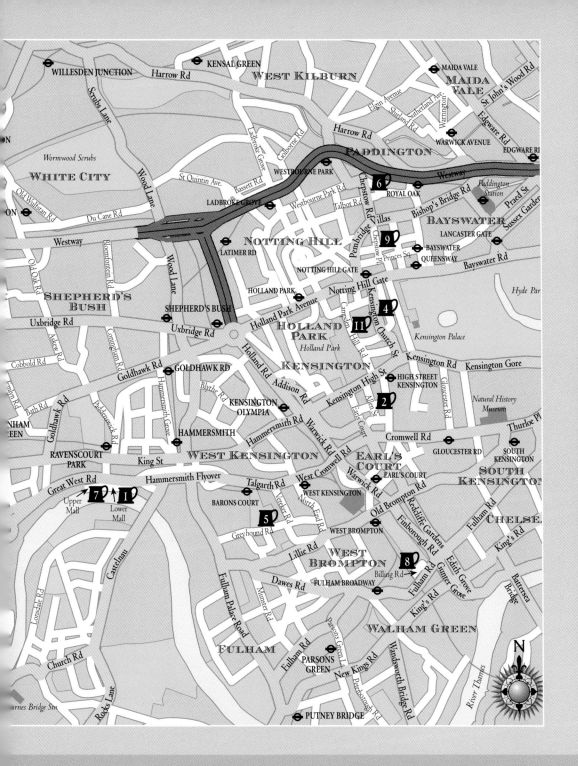

WILLESDEN JUNCTION
Harrow Rd
KENSAL GREEN
WEST KILBURN
MAIDA VALE
MAIDA VALE
Scrubs Lane
Elgin Avenue
Shirland Rd
Sutherland Ave.
Warrington
St John's Wood Rd
Edgware Rd
WARWICK AVENUE
EDGWARE RI
Harrow Rd
WESTBOURNE PARK
PADDINGTON
Westway
Praed St
Sussex Garden
Wormwood Scrubs
St Quintin Ave.
Bassett Rd
Ladbroke Grove
Golborne Rd
Westbourne Park Rd
Chepstow Rd
6
ROYAL OAK
Bishop's Bridge Rd
Paddington Station
BAYSWATER
WHITE CITY
Wood Lane
Du Cane Rd
LADBROKE GROVE
Talbot Rd
Pembridge Villas
9
LANCASTER GATE
Old Wulfstan Rd
Westway
Bloemfontein Rd
LATIMER RD
NOTTING HILL
NOTTING HILL GATE
Chepstow Pl.
Princes Sq
BAYSWATER
QUEENSWAY
Bayswater Rd
Hyde Par
SHEPHERD'S BUSH
Wood Lane
SHEPHERD'S BUSH
Uxbridge Rd
Uxbridge Rd
HOLLAND PARK
Holland Park Avenue
Notting Hill Gate
Camden Hill Rd
Kensington Church St
4
Kensington Palace
Cobbold Rd
Askew Rd
Coningham Rd
Goldhawk Rd
GOLDHAWK RD
Blythe Rd
Holland Rd
Addison Rd
HOLLAND PARK
Holland Park
KENSINGTON
11
Kensington Rd
Kensington Gore
Uxbridge Rd
Bath Rd
Goldhawk Rd
Paddenswick Rd
KENSINGTON OLYMPIA
Kensington High St
HIGH STREET KENSINGTON
2
Allan St.
Natural History Museum
Thurloe Pl
Goldhawk Rd
HAMMERSMITH
Hammersmith Grove
Hammersmith Rd
Warwick Rd
Earls Court
Cromwell Rd
GLOUCESTER RD
Gloucester Rd
SOUTH KENSINGTON
RAVENSCOURT PARK
King St
WEST KENSINGTON
EARL'S COURT
EARL'S COURT
SOUTH KENSINGTON
Great West Rd
Hammersmith Flyover
Talgarth Rd
West Cromwell Rd
Warwick Rd
7
1
Upper Mall
Lower Mall
BARONS COURT
Verker Rd
North End Rd
WEST KENSINGTON
Old Brompton Rd
Redcliffe Gardens
Finborough Rd
Fulham Rd
CHELSE
King's Rd
Castelnau
5
Greyhound Rd
WEST BROMPTON
Edith Grove
Gunter Grove
Lillie Rd
WEST BROMPTON
8
Billing Rd
King's Rd
Battersea Bridge
Church Rd
Lonsdale Rd
Rocks Lane
Fulham Palace Road
Munster Rd
Dawes Rd
FULHAM BROADWAY
WALHAM GREEN
FULHAM
Fulham Rd
PARSONS GREEN
Parsons Green L.
New Kings Rd
Wandsworth Bridge Rd
Peterborough Rd
N
Barnes Bridge Stn.
PUTNEY BRIDGE
River Thames

WEST LONDON 153

Blue Anchor

13 Lower Mall, Hammersmith W6 9DJ

BEERS: Four real ales always on tap and five premium lagers

Although tables sprawl outside, inside is far more intimate; the location makes it an ideal starting or finishing point for a walk along the north bank of the River Thames

As one would expect of a riverside pub situated between the Oxford and Cambridge Boat Race start by Putney Bridge and the race's finish at Mortlake, the Blue Anchor is a rowing pub. It is a smallish pub downstairs which maximizes its space with an upstairs room, from which there are great views of the river. There is also bench seating outside. You are informed as you enter that this tile-fronted building has been licensed since 1722 and that Gustav Holst (who was director of music at St Paul's Girls' School in nearby Brook Green) wrote the Hammersmith Suite here. It is unlikely that the pub has changed much since Holst's day.

Inside, the Blue Anchor has the feel of a rowing clubhouse: blades, oars and a boat hang from the ceiling of the wood-panelled interior. Its rowing atmosphere led to its use as a location in the film Sliding Doors starring John Hannah, who played a rower, and Gwyneth Paltrow. Walls are adorned with an interesting range of prints, though the work of local photographer Scott Thompson predominates. Pride of place goes to an antique beer engine in the front window (see also the Nags Head, p.108).

Naturally, the pub affords a superb view of the river. Playing fields belonging to St Paul's Boys' School are visible through the trees and to the left is Hammersmith Bridge. Heading west it is possible to enjoy a riverside walk that takes you past the Fuller's Brewery in Chiswick, the last big London brewery. From there you can walk on to Chiswick House, home of Lord Burlington of Royal Academy fame, and William Hogarth's house, which, ironically, is hard against the wall of Burlington's estate: Hogarth loathed Burlington's Palladian tastes for being very un-English. Over Hammersmith Bridge is the Wetlands Centre, an exceptional wildlife reserve in central London, built on 105 acres of the former Barnes reservoirs.

Britannia

1 Allen Street, Kensington W8 6UX

BEERS: Young's Bitter, Young's Special, Young's Triple A

The Britannia is a deceptively large pub, with an exceptional collection of political and satirical cartoons

Kensington is both an ancient settlement and a young part of London. Recorded in the Domesday Book of 1086 as Chenesit, the region just to the north of Kensington High Street from The Britannia has been a settlement ever since. At one time a manor of the Earls of Oxford, in the 17th century it became a popular place for the aristocracy to build large mansions as it offered all the advantages of a country seat within easy reach of London. The area received the royal imprimatur in 1689 when William III commissioned Sir Christopher Wren and others to convert Nottingham House into Kensington Palace.

Kensington has, therefore, always been a wealthy area, and, ever since the Temperance campaigns of the 19th century effectively divorced pubs from upper- and middle-class patronage, pubs in rich neighbourhoods were increasingly to be found in the backstreets for the exclusive use of tradesmen and servants.

The Britannia sits on Allen Street, which was named after a tailor, Thomas Allen, who made a fortune supplying military uniforms during the Napoleonic wars and then turned his hand to property development in the area – although not in Allen Street itself, which stayed as garden ground until around 1893. The area was also home to the Britannia Brewery, and the Allen Street pub was one of only two tied pubs this unsuccessful firm ever managed to secure, the other being the Britannia Tap in Warwick Road. The firm went bankrupt in 1902, and was rescued only to collapse again in 1924 when it was bought out by Young's. The pub was originally known as The Britannia Brewery Tap, shortening its name only in 1938. The present building dates back to 1834, although it was remodelled in 1959–60.

The walls of most London pubs are worthy of inspection, but the prints on display at The Britannia are of a superior quality altogether, with a fair sprinkling of Gillrays and Rowlandsons for the aficionados, and a few H. M. Batemans in the conservatory. Kensington High Street is very much dedicated to shoppers, but there are other attractions too. At Earls Court lies the Commonwealth Institute and on Kensington Gore – which takes its name from the old English 'gara', a triangular piece of land left when ploughing irregularly shaped fields – are the Albert Memorial and Royal Albert Hall.

The Bulls Head

15 Strand on the Green, Chiswick W4 3PQ

BEERS: Theakston's Best, Theakston's XB, Morland's Old Speckled Hen

A popular pub since the English Civil War (1642–49), particularly with those who enjoy hearty meals and walks along the Thames Path

It is fashionable to decry as a terrible cliché the claim that London is a series of villages that happen to have bumped into each other. Nevertheless, the portion of Chiswick known as Strand-on-the-Green, bordering the River Thames, is a perfect example of London village life. It is even unlikely that the residents acknowledge that they are in London, and they probably do not have to either, for the area isolated by the Thames to the south and the A4/M4 to the north is one that the vast majority of Londoners never visit.

Hence Strand-on-the-Green is a great retreat for people who want to escape London without the motorway misery this normally entails.

Escape is very much a theme at The Bulls Head. Its most famous customer, Oliver Cromwell, was a regular visitor during the English Civil War (1642–49) as his sister Mary, the Duchess of Fauconberg, was a local resident and benefactor. Betrayed to Royalist troops on one occasion, Cromwell escaped from The Bulls Head by a secret tunnel to Oliver's Eyot, the island in the Thames that sits opposite the inn. This island is the first of a surprisingly large number of islands in the Thames, some of which are inhabited. Visiting the pub today one cannot but feel that the Royalist troops were not especially bright or, more probably, not keen to get wet, because the eyot does seem a rather obvious place to look for a recently flown bird.

Appearances can be deceptive and The Bulls Head is a good example of this truism. The core fabric of the building is some 350 years old, but over the years it has expanded to incorporate adjoining cottages, and successive interior decorators have conspired to make it hard to see the joins. The pub is deceptively large, with an abundance of nooks and crannies, all on different levels and all given over to dining, making this a destination pub for Sunday lunches in particular. Work up an appetite with a walk along the riverside, or you could cross the river at Kew Bridge and take in the myriad delights of Kew Gardens. Serious walkers could press on along the north bank to Syon Park.

The Churchill Arms

119 Kensington Church Street, Kensington W8 7LN

BEERS: Fuller's Chiswick Bitter, Fuller's London Pride, Fuller's ESB

This pub in a quiet corner of Kensington is divided into a number of sections, each jammed full of ephemera of frequently bizarre origin

One might suspect that the landlord of The Churchill Arms is a little bit potty, since there are no fewer than 101 chamber pots hanging on the ceiling. This is certainly one of London's more oddball pubs, and yet in its eccentricity it is truly endearing. The dominant theme is Sir Winston Churchill – portraits of him abound; books by him and about him can be taken down from the shelves; and there is much to learn about this extraordinary man, who clearly believed that destiny had marked him for greatness at a very early age. Churchill takes centre stage in a pantheon of British prime ministers, from Walpole to Wilson, occupying one wall. Meanwhile, in the other arm of the pub a similar compliment is paid to American presidents, from Washington to Nixon.

The pub is divided into distinct areas. To the left of the bar, complete with original snob screens (which along with the number of doors to the street indicate that the pub was once divided into three areas) is the potty/presidents' area. In front of the bar potties give way to hat boxes. To the right of the bar are prime ministers, pots, lanterns and varied hanging ephemera. There is a further area and food servery hidden behind the chimney brace – this is the baskets and butterflies department; some 1,600 butterflies are carefully mounted and framed.

Finally, there is the conservatory dining area, the walls of which are a riot of colour and whose ceiling is a tangle of trailing tendrils from hundreds of pot plants. Thai food is very much the theme here, and the feeling is one of eating in the jungle. To complete the mêlée there's landlord Gerry O'Brien: his name alone is explanation for the Irish flavour, for those of you scratching your heads trying to recall Churchill's Irish connections.

The pub was originally called The Marlborough after Churchill's ancestor and victor of the Battle of Blenheim. Oddly, no mention of him appears now.

The Colton Arms

187 Greyhound Road, London W14 9SD

BEERS: Changing ales

A village pub serving a village that happens to be in a city

Norman and Dorothy Nunn took over the tenancy at the Colton Arms in 1965. They changed very little at this old Watney's house, keeping much of the décor that had been accumulated by the previous landlord but one at the end of Second World War. Wonderful décor it is too.

Heavy carved oak settles, horse brasses and lots of copper and china knick-knacks arranged around a mock-Tudor interior invite a double-take as you step from the typically West London aspect of Greyhound Road into an archetypal country village inn.

Jonathan Nunn continues to run the pub following his parents' retirement, having joined them on the licence – he was working for Beefeater Gin – in 1988. Since then he has seen the neighbourhood change dramatically. What was once quite an industrial area has been made entirely residential and has been gentrified to boot.

As a consequence the impression is that the Colton has become stuck in a time warp as it now keeps traditional opening hours. Older readers may recall that it was only on 1st August 1988 that the British government noticed that the First World War appeared to have come to a conclusion and relaxed the draconian restrictions on pub opening hours that were introduced in order to boost the manufacture of artillery ammunition. With the decline of business trade during the day, and being that very rare creature these days – a pub that doesn't serve food – the Colton has retreated to more traditional opening times, including closing during the afternoons at weekends. You are advised to check before you visit to avoid disappointment.

The pub's name reflects the area's industrial past. George Colton was a clay pipe maker from across town in Hoxton who relocated to Fulham, it is assumed, sometime in the 1790s. A pair of visiting historians set Jonathan to rooting around in the attic and, sure enough, he found fragments of clay pipe.

Clientele are a cross section of local Fulham life: 'boys from the village' checking the racing form to the slightly more Sloaney types who have moved in to the neighbourhood in recent years. They all, however, appreciate the special nature of the Colton. A fixed star in a changing universe; an island of tranquility in a sea of madness; one of London's great pubs.

The Cow

89 Westbourne Park Road, Westbourne Park W2 5QH

BEERS: Fuller's London Pride, Uley Bitter plus weekly guest ale

This characterful dining pub has a strong Belgian feel in its beers and menu, blended with a traditional oysters-and-stout theme long-forgotten in most pubs

On a bench in The Mayflower, Rotherhithe (see pp.208–209), is a quotation from Charles Dickens to the effect that poverty and oysters always go together. At The Cow in Westbourne Park, which styles itself a 'saloon bar and dining rooms', this is demonstrably untrue. Admittedly, they maintain the old custom of serving oysters with Guinness, but the customers of the Cow are not London's working classes. Oysters were a working-class staple in Dickens time, rather than the luxury they are today. Tons and tons of them would have travelled up the Thames from the Whitstable oyster beds to feed the London poor – who would also have drunk porter as their staple liquid intake and another important source of nutrition. Guinness is more properly a stout, but stout is a type of porter and true porter is barely produced today.

The Cow is owned by Tom Conran, who also owns the Lucky Seven a few doors down. When you enter the Cow you may be a little unsure as to where you are or which suburb of Brussels you have landed in. The ambience is decidedly Belgian: the menus are up on mirrors over the dining area; the emphasis is 'gastronomique', and seafood, which lends the whole place the aroma of lemons, is of prime importance, with an ice bar in pride of place keeping fresh the day's stock of oysters, crab and shellfish. It's not all Belgian all the time, though, as there is a feel also of Irish pubs and French brasseries about the place.

There is a dining room upstairs which is renowned for its choice of oysters. The Cow's

motto is 'Eat heartily and give the house a good name,' which is a pretty Belgian sentiment too. Nearby attractions include the Portobello Road street market, and August Bank Holiday weekend sees the famous Notting Hill Carnival take over the entire neighbourhood. The seating outside the Cow makes an ideal spot from which to watch the party.

The Dove

19 Upper Mall, Hammersmith W6 9TA

BEERS: Fuller's Oliver's Island Fuller's London Pride, Fuller's ESB

You begin to step back in time as soon as you near the Dove and the narrow flagstone path that approaches it; once inside, try to squeeze into the country's smallest bar

What do the composer Khatchaturian, the novelists Graham Greene and Ernest Hemingway, and the actors Richard Burton and Rex Harrison have in common? They have all frequented The Dove. This is one of London's premier taverns and it exudes history from its very timbers. On the north bank of the River Thames the pub is known as The Dove, on the south or Surrey side it is known as The Doves as a result of an error on an inn sign facing the river in the 1860s.

The main claim to fame (although it has been contested) of the otherwise largely forgotten poet James Thomson is that he wrote the old Proms favourite 'Rule, Britannia', and he did this at The Dove. However, he also took a boat from The Dove, caught a chill and died. For a full list of celebrities who have passed some time there consult the mantelpiece over the fire in the front bar, where perhaps a couple of hundred names are listed.

William Morris, the writer and Arts and Crafts designer, lived next door – his house is now a museum. A. P. Herbert used The Dove as a model for The Pigeons in his novel *The Water Gipsies*, and Charles II and Nell Gwyn are said to have enjoyed a drink here. Royalty that definitely did drink at The Dove includes Queen Victoria's uncle Augustus Frederick, Duke of Sussex, who used to retire to the house next door – No. 17, once part of the same property – which he referred to as his 'smoking box'. Here, the duke would sit and contemplate the river and plan strategies for the campaign closest to his heart, the abolition of slavery.

Just to the right of the front door is The Dove's other claim to fame – England's smallest bar. The room measures a mere four feet two inches wide, which is 'snug' by any definition of the word. The pub offers a tremendous view of the river as it turns south towards Mortlake and really does invite you to resume the river walk and think Jerome K. Jerome-type thoughts.

The Fox & Pheasant

1 Billing Road, Chelsea SW10 9UJ

BEERS: Greene King IPA, Greene King Abbot Ale

This 'country' pub in the heart of Fulham is a haven for football lovers, being only minutes from Stamford Bridge.

The Fox & Pheasant takes its influence from the three delightful Georgian terraces that comprise Billing Street and Billing Terrace. These are notable for their delicate pastel-painted houses which make you wonder how many watercolourists must have set up easel in this little oasis under the shadow of Ken Bates's football club-cum-lifestyle complex at Stamford Bridge, home to Chelsea Football Club.

If your idea of a lifestyle complex is a decent boozer then the Fox & Pheasant is likely to fit the bill. A simple two-bar pub with a clever office-style bar reminiscent of those 'lazy s' shaped lovers' seats that enable you to sit next to but facing your paramour. It enables the public and saloon bars to be separate yet served and overseen by just one member of staff. The public bar, naturally, is the sparser of the two yet tends to be the more popular. It opens out to a walled garden that is a real suntrap, enabling you to relax, soak up the heat and completely forget that you are only in SW10.

If you turn right on entering the pub you will find yourself in the saloon, which has a fairly traditional alehouse interior of half-panelling below nicotine-coloured walls.

The pub is only a few yards off the Fulham Road, which has been a major London thoroughfare since the 15th century, when it was called the King's Highway or the London Road. Famous Fulham Road residents have included the writer Arnold Bennett and textile designer Laura Ashley, though whether they visited the Fox & Pheasant is not known (certainly, Ashley's influence is not in evidence).

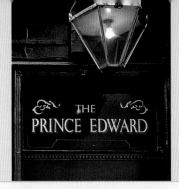

The Prince Edward

73 Princes Square, Westbourne Grove W2 4NY

BEERS: Fox, plus guest ales

Bustling community pub with interesting collections of ephemera and excellent Hall & Woodhouse beers

A few moments away from the bustle of Bayswater this large, street corner place feels like a friendly country pub in the centre of London. Built in the mid 19th century the Prince Edward is located on the west side of a leafy Victorian Square. A community pub, some of its customers have been drinking here for over 40 years while others have just arrived in the city and are staying in one of the many bustling hotels nearby.

A large, central bar dominates an open, high-ceilinged room, skilfully divided into several cosy areas each with a different eclectic feel. Art deco sits casually next to modern kitchen chic. Collections of butterflies, elephants, old prints, photographs, china curiosities and marvellous etched glass mirrors vie for attention; even the condiments, served in old chamber pots, are a cause for conversation. Outside there are plenty of places for drinkers to settle overlooked by a portrait of Prince Edward on the day of his coronation in 1902.

Back inside, the large, enveloping leather chairs are the perfect place to enjoy a pint of one of Hall & Woodhouse's understated beers whilst the large glass windows allow light to stream in. Hall and Woodhouse is an independent family brewer, founded in 1777, which is based in Blandford Forum in Dorset and the company has a handful of pubs in the capital – each with its own idiosyncratic character and identity, yet they are all united by the quality of the beer they serve.

After a refurbishment, there is now an underground function room and a proper restaurant area. It also claims to be the only pub in London to offer a Kobe burger. The meat comes from the UK's only herd of traditional Japanese Wagyu cattle, which have been given a welcome on the hills around Voelas Hall, in the Lleyn Peninsula, North Wales. Kobe is said to be the most succulent and tender meat in the world. The cattle have regular massages with sake, said to create truly contented beasts with meat that shows extraordinary marbling. Indeed, the herd live a life of luxury before they end up on the grill. They are fed a diet of grains and racehorse grass and hay supplemented with beer.

Prince Edward was known as the peacemaker, and his namesake pub, is certainly the place at certain times of the day for a relaxing drink. But it can be a busy world too and full of conversation and laughter.

The Tabard

Bath Road, Chiswick W4 1LW

BEERS: 30 different rotating ales

This superb Arts and Crafts pub is an architectural treasure and a refreshing change from the plentiful Victorian pubs in London

The Arts and Crafts movement of the late 19th century has left a surprisingly small footprint on London, and considering that it coincided with a period of frantic pub building there are surprisingly few Arts and Crafts pubs in London. The Tabard, however, is one such. Built in 1880 by the architect Norman Shaw it forms part of the 24-acre development founded by Jonathan Carr that was to be known as Bedford Park. It was Carr's idea to create a middle-class commuting village, made possible by the opening of Turnham Green tube station in 1869, and Bedford Park became the first of what were known as the 'garden suburbs'.

Carr's ambitions were very much in line with the philosophy of the Arts and Crafts movement, and the area attracted aesthetes and politically minded free thinkers. A tabard, as the inn sign by the painter T. M. Rorke depicts, is the tunic worn by a herald. However, the pub may well take its name from the Tabard Inn made famous by Geoffrey Chaucer in *The Canterbury Tales* which had been demolished by property developers in 1875 despite huge public opposition, and perhaps it was to keep the Chaucerian flag flying that the pub took the name.

The interior is unique, with Arts and Crafts tiles by William de Morgan covering the upper walls of the right-hand bar. These tiles are such a fine example of the movement's style that their counterparts are held by the British Museum. De Morgan was a disciple of the great Arts and Crafts pioneer and radical socialist William Morris, and Morris's influence is very much in evidence. Further tiles, by the artist Walter Crane, in an avant-garde style

that would eventually become Art Nouveau, are on display around the fireplace to the left of the bar. The porch, too, is original and the present occupiers have been careful to ensure that the shape and style of furniture and fittings are sympathetic to the building's distinctive lines.

In line with Bedford Park's artistic origins The Tabard boasts its own theatre, which is accessed from the pub's garden. Bedford Park boasts buildings by a number of famous architects, including E. W. Godwin, C. F. A. Voysey and Maurice Adams. W. B. Yeats's family lived there, and G. K. Chesterton knew it well, too.

Nowadays, the pub is very community-based, running an activities club for local elderly residents every Tuesday.

Windsor Castle

114 Campden Hill Road, Kensington W8 7AR

BEERS: Meantime Fool's Gold, Beavertown Gamma Ray, Blanche De Bruxelles, Lagunita New DogTown

This old alehouse has the air of the countryside about it, but sits in the heart of fashionable Kensington

It is unlikely that there is any truth in the story that the Windsor Castle got its name because on a clear day it was possible to see Windsor Castle from Campden Hill. However, once inside the pub, looking out of the window is likely to be fairly low down your 'to do' list, as this magnificent early Victorian boozer is a real feast for the eyes.

The Windsor Castle must contain one of the least altered Victorian interiors in London. It is still partitioned by fairly solid wood screens, into which are set tiny interconnecting doors. These doors were intended for use by bar staff and cleaners and not customers, which is why they were discreetly small. Customers were expected to exit the pub and re-enter by another door if they wished to change drinking area. (Today, only the Prince Alfred in Maida Vale can boast similar features, but this has been turned into a bistro. Hopefully one day someone will restore it to its proper status and glory.)

Each of the doors into the Windsor Castle bears its own legend. There is the Campden Bar, the Private Bar and, intriguingly, the Sherry Bar. The latter is a reference to the pub's sadly extinct tradition of serving a drink called the Hunter, which is a bit like a Bloody Mary but with sherry rather than vodka.

Beautifully dingy, the Windsor Castle has lots of original dark wood, settles and rustic benches, which only add to the warm feeling that would have been so important in attracting custom in the days when escaping the cold was of rather more significance than it is today. In warmer weather, a pleasant garden area is also open. The pub is within easy walking distance of Portobello Road Market, Kensington Gardens and Holland Park.

SOUTHWEST LONDON

Southwest London is the fiefdom of those most admirable of fellows, Young's. Until September 2006, when Young's closed their brewery site and merged with Bedford brewer Charles Wells, there had been a brewery in Wandsworth since 1581, so it is not surprising that Young's managed to claim the region as their own. Young's pubs still operate as

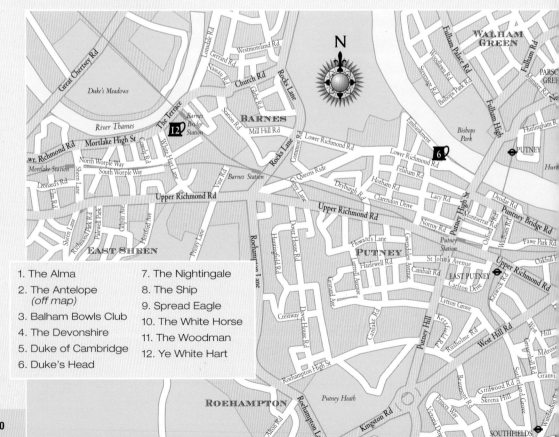

1. The Alma
2. The Antelope (off map)
3. Balham Bowls Club
4. The Devonshire
5. Duke of Cambridge
6. Duke's Head
7. The Nightingale
8. The Ship
9. Spread Eagle
10. The White Horse
11. The Woodman
12. Ye White Hart

a separate company, however, and given Young's unfashionably dogged determination to do things the traditional way, southwest London is a rich treasure trove of delightful public houses. From the first entry in this chapter through to the last, you will be assured of a perfect pint of bitter whichever Young's establishment you choose. However, Young's do not always have it their own way, and there are enough superb non-Young's pubs south of the river to ensure that the chaps from Wandsworth are kept on their toes.

The Alma

499 Old York Road, Wandsworth SW18 1TF

BEERS: Young's Bitter, Young's Special

The central bar is now the main focus in this redesigned Victorian pub, where an eclectic collection of furniture and brightly painted tables create a cheerful, relaxed atmosphere

On the outside The Alma is an inspiring and handsome mid-Victorian London pub, on the inside a French fin-de-siècle bistro. Built in 1866, it takes its name from nearby Alma Road and Alma Cottages, which were built around 1854 at the time of the Battle of the Alma in the Crimean War.

The big open lounge room is a mix of features and styles. The large central bar is a hotchpotch of many styles, whilst on the walls are three unique mosaic

roundels featuring the pub's name. The corner area around the broad wooden stairs is beautifully decorated with painted mirrors, which are just right for the period (mid-19th centruy) and extremely rare. Further mirrors in the little alcove under the stairs are reminiscent of other fine examples found in The Washington (see p.149) in Primrose Hill. The gallic feel of the pub is accentuated by the choice of furniture, an old cool box, a picture of a French village square, and painted tables.

To the rear is a dining room serving superb-quality modern pub cooking – the Alma is well-known for it locally. Here the main feature is a rustic table of immense proportions, and the room also boasts a decorative plaster frieze that had previously been hidden and was only discovered during renovation in 1987.

Being some 200 yards from the site of the old Young's Brewery, this – like pretty much every pub in SW18 – is naturally a Young's house, serving the brewery's widely respected ales. Young's merged with respected Bedford brewers Charles Wells in 2007, creating a new force in the industry, Wells & Young's Brewing Company Ltd, though its pubs still operate as a separate company. The Young's brewery itself was a major attraction in the area until its closure.

Being perfectly situated on Old York Road with its delightful villagey atmosphere, The Alma is an excellent stop-off after a Saturday morning jaunt to the bustling little farmer's market outside Wandsworth Town station, which it is opposite.

The Antelope

76 Mitcham Road, London SW17 9NG

BEERS: Dark Star Hophead, Sharp's Doom Bar, plus changing guest ales and Volden house beer

High Victorian luxury with a focus on comfortable surroundings

The pub company Antic takes its name from its somewhat eccentric founder Anthony Thomas. A much better name for the company would be SPOP – the Society for the Protection of Old Pubs. The number of Antic pubs seems to multiply faster than a warren of rabbits, but a significant proportion of them – excluding the ones that are imaginative re-usings of unwanted old post offices and job centres – are honest to goodness old London boozers that had fallen out of favour and just needed a little love to be set back on their feet again. The Antelope is one such.

This large, wood-panelled, Edwardian, ex-Barclay Perkins pub must have been quite an imposing presence on the Mitcham Road in its heyday. Originally known as the Foresters Arms, licence records have a pub on the site from at least 1871. It later became known as Jack Beards after a John (Jack) Beard who became landlord in 1891. The pub stayed in his large family till at least 1917 as he was merely the first of a number of Beards on the licence, followed into the trade by wife Catherine and then daughters and sons Lilly, Arthur, Florence, Maud and John.

In its latter days Jack Beards had become rather grey. There was a boxing ring upstairs which hosted illegal matches and had become a rather insalubrious gambling den before its inevitable demise and the pub's closure. It was rescued and restored by Antic and reopened in July 2009. It has lots of original features, especially the large U-shaped bar, but the wood panelling throughout is what lends it both grandeur and atmosphere, especially in the large function room to the left and the always immaculately laid out restaurant to the right at the rear.

The pub is therefore naturally suited to holding functions. Weddings are often held here, and, in the winter especially, it must rate as one of the best spots in London to take Sunday lunch. Food and drink are both sourced locally where possible and the kitchen aims to champion the best of Britain in a neighbourhood that is teeming with Indian and Lebanese influences. It must rate as one of the jewels in Antic's crown and under its present management team is currently on a roll.

Balham Bowls Club

7–9 Ramsden Road, London SW12 8QX

BEERS: Changing range of guest ales

A terrific example of how a new use can be found for an old building

In Forest Hill the Sylvan Post is a friendly local that used to be the post office. You drink in the vaults. The Effra Social in Brixton is the old Conservative Club. You can raise a toast to a portrait or the queen. And in Deptford the Job Centre used to be, er, a job centre. All of these are imaginative reworkings of

redundant and unloved buildings and all belong to the Antic pub company (see the Antelope pp.174–175 and the Royal Albert pp.212–213). However, the revitalised building with unquestionably the best linger power is the Balham Bowls Club.

There's a clue in the title. It used to be a bowling club, and it's in Balham. When Antic took it on some six years ago, many of the trappings and paraphernalia of the club were still on the premises and these form the basis of the fascinating and superbly laid out décor. The building still retains its fantastic 1930s interior (the club was actually founded in 1893) and the original function of each of the extensive suite of spacious rooms is still apparent.

Upstairs is a large ballroom, again with lots of original features. A shade tatty, perhaps, but that is very much the Antic style. It takes no leap of the imagination to imagine what the place was like in its heyday, with the bar thronged with ladies and gents dressed in their whites after an enjoyable afternoon on the lawns. Regimental badges from men with a military bearing still festoon the bar. What better way to finish off the day than by retiring into the front parlour for a rubber or two of bridge.

If you wonder where the lawns were, well, they are still there. They're hidden behind the fence in the corner of the garden, home now to foxes and hedgehogs rather than retired colonels. Of course when it was a club you had to be a member to get in. Today, thanks to Antic, you don't.

The Devonshire

39 Balham High Road, Balham SW12 9AN

BEERS: Young's Bitter, Young's Special, Charles Wells Bombardier

The Devonshire, Balham's pride, has one of London's 'don't miss' pub interiors – opulence embodied; its modest location on Balham High Road gives little away about the architectural finery that lies within

Since its early days as a rural village, Balham has changed dramatically, and at last, so has the Devonshire. Formerly the Duke of Devonshire, the pub lost its title during its most recent makeover.

It still offers a warm welcome, high standards and a great atmosphere, but with added style, comfort and some seriously funky furniture. The kitchen, meanwhile, is open plan and features a Botticelli reproduction on one wall. The Devonshire is the most exciting thing to happen in Balham for quite some time.

Victorian music halls grew out of pubs of this size; a pub with the Duke of Devonshire name dates back to at least 1827. For many years it was a beer house only – that is, it didn't have a licence to sell spirits or wine. Beer houses were an attempt to substitute beer consumption (wholesome) for gin consumption (poisonous). Even so it was a very busy house. In 1857 it was doing some 613 butts of porter per annum – that's 1,450 pints a day. In order to serve this volume it's no wonder that the bar at the Devonshire is so massive. Shaped like a giant G-clamp, it is some 45 yards in length, and behind it is a sumptuous array of etched glass. This is very much in the style that became known as gin palace, though real gin palaces were actually much plainer.

Not all the windows in the Devonshire are original, but the later ones are still handsome and do not detract from the gin palace style. Sadly, electric light can never recapture the true feel of gas, but it requires no great leap of imagination to recreate the magnificence of the Devonshire in the muggy days of gas lighting. An interior like this cannot fail to stimulate the mind.

Duke of Cambridge

228 Battersea Bridge Road, Battersea SW11 3AA

BEERS: Young's Bitter, Young's Special, Young's Triple A

The style of the Duke of Cambridge is very modern yet full of character and interest; the pub itself dates from Victoria's reign

Walking into the Duke of Cambridge is a bit like walking into a David Hockney picture: lots of bold colours and strong lines and an immediately striking impression. The brainchild of Nick Elliot and Joanne Clevely, who cut their teeth at The Chelsea Ram and The Queens in Regent's Park Road, this is an example of how to take an old pub and give it a sympathetically contemporary slant.

One of six Dukes owing fealty to Young's Brewery, this particular establishment was built in the early 1860s when Battersea was rapidly developed as a result of the construction of Battersea Bridge. The pub's stables were once home to a volunteer fire crew in the days before the foundation of the London Fire Brigade. They were also used by the No. 34 omnibus from Islington to Battersea, one of the last horse-drawn buses in London, which, of course, was killed off by the arrival of the railway at Nine Elms in 1838 and Clapham Junction in 1846.

The duke himself, whose photograph adorns a wall, was very much an animal-rights activist. In 1886 he instituted the London Cart Horse Parade in Battersea Park, the objectives of which were – and still are – to improve the general condition and treatment of London's cart horses, to encourage drivers to take a human interest in the animals under their care, and to encourage the wider use of powerful cart horses on London's streets. Between 1888 and 1994 the parade took place in Regent's Park, and from 1995–2006 the London Harness Horse Parade moved back to its original home a few yards from the Duke of Cambridge. Now held at the South of England Centre in West Sussex, the parade takes place every Easter Monday. Treasurer of the parade is J.G.A. Young – a fitting association as Young's delivered by horse and dray, within a one-mile radius of the old brewery, until 2006.

Much to be admired is the mural to the rear of the pub by the artist Paul Karslake. All the regulars are featured, and the masterful painting required an impressive spatial awareness by the artist, painting a scene both in reverse and from a point of view that he could not see. The daily changing menu makes this a seriously good food pub and the general confidence and ease of touch with which the whole place is run marks it out as first-class.

Duke's Head

8 Lower Richmond Road, Putney SW15 1JN

BEERS: Young's Bitter, Young's Special, Charles Wells Bombardier

The Duke's Head is always packed in April for the annual Boat Race, but the pub's good river views from a salon-style setting means that it's pretty busy every other day of the year, too

The original 1832 Duke's Head was rebuilt in 1864 and further altered in 1894, but has always been in the Young's Brewery portfolio.

It has the kind of London pub interior that no one would manage to look after quite as well as Young's. The Duke's Head has something for

every taste. The lads and locals will congregate in the back bar, furthest from the river, while the main action is on the river side. The principal

hustle and bustle takes place in the front dining room, which affords river views on three sides, including the best view of the start of the Oxford and Cambridge Boat Race. Downstairs there is a newly opened basement bar.

Almost as busy is the area round the elaborate and original bar. Island bars were very much a mid-Victorian innovation and owe their invention to the famous engineer Isambard Kingdom Brunel. Passengers on Brunel's Great Western Railway often faced a short but necessary wait at Swindon, and the railway's bar was too small to serve all the thirsty customers before it was time for the porters to shout 'all aboard' once more. Brunel realized that a round 'island' bar maximized the available bar frontage in relation to the number of people waiting and staff serving, meaning that more people could be served in the same time with less frustration.

The idea caught on and boosted the trend of the 1870s and 1880s for pubs to be divided into rooms and snugs. Privacy soon became the main theme, and, with the improvement in acid-etching techniques, frosted glass and snob screens became the order of the day.

Towards the end of the century licensing magistrates reacted against the increasing complexity of this fashion, favouring greater supervision and visibility (they were paranoid about prostitutes and pickpockets plying their trades). Pubs were forced to reduce the number of rooms they had and many island bars went, literally, to the wall.

The Nightingale

97 Nightingale Lane, Clapham SW12 8NX

BEERS: Young's Bitter, Young's Special, Sambrook's Wandle, Sharp's Doom Bar, plus guests

The Nightingale's appealing exterior and interior draw in a broad spectrum of Balham and Clapham's populace

Nightingale Lane was originally known as Balham Wood Lane, and no one is sure whether the pub is named after the lane or the lane after the pub, or whether the truth lies elsewhere – with those who maintain that the area was once noted for nightingales' song.

The pub was built in a deliberately unpub-like style as part of the disposal of the Old Park Estate which was sold in lots in 1869. The estate owners clearly had views on what sort of a neighbourhood should be created by the developers of this previously rural area. For example, they stipulated that no house could be sold for less than £800 and that no house should be within 25 feet of the road.

The Nightingale has been a Young's pub since 1920. Today it is widely respected and is definitely a good, reliable local. It is also a versatile house catering for a number of different types of clientele at different times of day. Lunchtime sees the old boys nursing a leisurely pint but also quite brisk trade from the surprisingly large number of office workers hidden in this ostensibly residential neighbourhood. In the evenings the average age drops slightly as people return from work in central London.

The Nightingale's interior is very much in the Young's style with rich wood hues, with a relatively low ceiling (by London standards), all inter-acting to suffuse this single-roomed pub with a cosy welcoming glow.

A good clue to the community nature of the Nightingale are photographs of the annual Nightingale Walk, which is a long-running community charity event.

The Ship

41 Jews Row, Wandsworth SW18 1TB

BEERS: Young's Bitter, Young's Special, Young's Triple A

This gastro pub has a trendy young professional clientèle that is attracted to the fine dining, well-kept beers, great beer garden and riverside location offered by the Ship – what more could they ask for?

The sister pub to The Alma (see pp.172–173) – they share the same management team – The Ship is in a similar mould but on a grander scale. A riverside pub with a large outdoor area and a great atmosphere, it has views of the river that, although they don't really compare with those from the Duke's Head, are decidedly better than in years gone by when a row of cottages existed between the river and the pub. The brewery bought the cottages in 1848 with the express intent of knocking them down.

The main part of the building, dating back to 1809 and first leased by Young's in 1832, is the least used part – the front bar can be empty while the riverside bar is thronging. The focus of the pub is all in the conservatory, which was added only in 1988. One side is a proper restaurant serving modern British cuisine of a standard that makes it advisable to book.

In recent years a permanent barbecue has been built to serve the outdoor trade, and there is even a summer bar – Doolali – in a beach-bar-type shack to cope with the considerable seasonal trade the pub attracts. The clientèle is predominantly young professional, and is likely to remain so given the amount of 'executive' apartment building that has gone on and is set to continue in the neighbourhood.

Riverside walking to the east is not possible, but to the west things are improving, allowing you to take in Wandsworth Park on the way to Putney. Nearby attractions include the Hurlingham Club and Bishop's Park.

Spread Eagle

71 Wandsworth High Street, Wandsworth SW18 2PT

BEERS: Young's Bitter, Young's Special, Young's Triple A

The Spread Eagle is a superb example of the grand Victorian pub, complete with fine glasswork and a spacious bar

Among the declining band of authentic Victorian pub interiors the Spread Eagle could clearly claim aristocratic status. Grandeur is the word that springs to mind as soon as you enter this large, imposing space, and grandeur was what was in the forefront of the minds of the designers. The sheer extent of the glasswork in the pub is magnificent. The Spread Eagle was certainly thought of as grand by the well-to-do of Wandsworth society in the late 19th century.

The pub was in existence prior to 1780, and by 1836, when it was acquired by Young's, it was already an important coaching inn and therefore very much part of the commercial centre of Wandsworth. Magistrates would meet there and various civic functions took place, including the first meeting of the proprietors of Surrey Iron Railway. It is impressive to consider that the Spread Eagle was considerably more extensive in the mid-19th century than today. The brewery property book of 1857 states that 'these premises occupy a commanding position in the High Street with considerable frontage in Garratt Lane. They consist of a tavern and tea garden, a large ballroom, a portion of which is now used as the County Court, a separate tap which has a licence of its own and a considerable range of stabling.'

In later years and until 1890 the Assembly Rooms on this site were used for music-hall acts and then became one of London's first bioscope cinemas. The 19th-century features visible today date from the complete rebuilding of the pub in 1898, when much of the extra space was disposed of. The old Young's Brewery site is just across the street.

The White Horse

Parson's Green Lane, Fulham SW6 4UL

BEERS: Harveys Sussex Bitter, Fuller's London Pride, Adnams Broadside, plus 5 guests

Dedicated to quality beers, the White Horse is a class apart when it comes to training and education

Housed within a grand Victorian building at the northern point of Parsons Green, and known affectionately as the Sloaney Pony, a coaching inn has existed on the site of the present White Horse since at least 1688. In that year John Haines, the then victualler of Ye Olde White Horse, was asked to appear before the local court baron for 'setting up posts before his house at Parsons Greene without leave of ye Lord of the Manor'. He was fined six shillings and eight pence and ordered 'that he remove them by the first of April next under the paine of twenty shillings'.

Close to Parsons Green underground station, the area owes its name to the parsonage or rectory that stood midway along the West side of the green. Reputedly the site of a vineyard in Roman times, this was by far the most aristocratic quarter of Fulham, inhabited mostly by 'gentry and persons of quality'.

The White Horse was also the meeting place of the old Fulham Albion Cricket Club, one of the pioneer cricket clubs in England.

After its latest and most extensive renovation, the White Horse created a dedicated dining area in what was the old coach house, doubled the size of its kitchens, modernised the lighting and decorated the walls using organic lime wash paints. The resulting space is a pleasing blend of traditional mahogany bar and wall panels, wood and flagstone floors, open fires and contemporary lighting. This is a busy pub, often with as many people outside in the beer garden as inside.

The White Horse has more than 135 bottled beers from around the world each of which is rated outstanding in its style category and deserves to be called world classic. Of particular note is the fact that it has gathered beers from six of the seven Trappist monasteries currently brewing as well as – a decade ago – being one of the first pubs to sell beers such as Budvar and Hoegaarden.

Placing an emphasis on training and education, the White Horse runs events such as Beer Academy Courses that focus on beer and food matching. It runs its own well-known Old Ale Festival, as well as quarterly beer festivals, and is the haunt of many brewers who frequently meet here for a pint when they are in London.

The Woodman

60 Battersea High Street, Battersea SW11 3HX

BEERS: Badger Best Bitter, Tanglefoot, King and Barnes Sussex

Brewers Hall and Woodhouse ensure that excellent beer is available at the front-of-house island bar, while out back a variety of games are on hand to ensure the Woodman has a relaxed and fun atmosphere

Mention the Woodman to most south Londoners and they will think of the pub with the table of board games, puzzles and parlour games. Just a few yards from trendy and village-like Battersea Square, this long, narrow Hall and Woodhouse pub was very much a yuppie hangout in the late 1980s. Yuppies have given way to 'dinkies', and a new generation of young couples now fill the Woodman.

The Woodman, with its blend of bright colours, snakeskin seats and modern art, goes on much as before, both as a good ale boozer and a fun pub. The front area, with its eccentrically shaped island bar, is suitably traditional and opens out to a long extension leading to an enclosed outdoor seating area. This is where you sit and frown in frustration as you attempt one of the games, be it negotiating a ball bearing through a maze while avoiding the traps, pulling one stick from a pile of sticks without disturbing the others, trying to expand the English language with a new seven-consonant word or vainly trying to keep your queen beyond move number five.

The pub was once one of the few London outlets for Hall and Woodhouse favourites such as Badger beer and Tanglefoot, and although these ales can be found in more and more pubs, The Woodman is still very much a promoter of the Dorset brewery.

Live music, fine ales, outdoor barbecues and a general fun atmosphere make this pub a good all-rounder with commendable cross-generational appeal and charm.

Ye White Hart

The Terrace, Riverside, Barnes SW13 0NR

BEERS: Young's Bitter, Young's Special, Young's Triple A

Ye White Hart has impressively spacious premises designed to take full advantage of the views of the River Thames

The White Hart is one of London's largest waterside pubs, commanding an impressive sweep of the river at the base of the Barnes reach as it curves northwards again towards Chiswick. It is a popular destination on a sunny day, and with seating on the terrace and below on the towpath it is capable of accommodating several hundred people without appearing crowded. Nevertheless, even Ye White Hart will get crowded on the day of the Oxford and Cambridge Boat Race as it offers one of the best vantage points of the race: unlike the Putney pubs such as the Duke's Head (see pp.182–183), the battle is often still being hard fought as the boats pass beneath the pub towards the finish at The Ship a quarter of a mile or so further upstream.

Established in 1662, Ye White Hart is one of the oldest pubs in this part of London. The first written reference to the inn is from 1676 (it was then known as The King's Arms) when, on the death of Robert Warner, a cooper, it passed to his son Charles. The pub stayed in the Warner family's hands until 1736. In 1766 it was acquired by the Trevy family of neighbouring Putney, who changed the name to Ye White Hart.

It entered the estate of the Wandsworth brewery firm of Young and Bainbridge, as Young's was originally known, in 1857, and towards the end of the 19th century it was extensively rebuilt, which resulted in its current exterior and appearance. The large balconies enabled the pub to capitalize on the bonanza that the Boat Race affords, and this also accounts for the balustrade running round the edge of the uncharacteristically flat roof.

Given the presence of the function room on the first floor, Ye White Hart is very much southwest London's answer to the Greenwich taverns that boasted large ballrooms on their upper floors, of which the Trafalgar Tavern (see pp.216–217) is the only survivor.

SOUTHEAST LONDON

Southeast London is probably the most diverse region in the city – Peckham, for example, sharing few similarities with its close neighbour, Dulwich. As such, it has a superb variety of pubs, from the Market Porter in the bustling thoroughfares of Borough to the Greenwich Union which sits in genteel backstreets. One regular feature, however, is the River Thames: once the major source of employment for the area's residents, it now forms the backdrop to a large number of the establishments selected here.

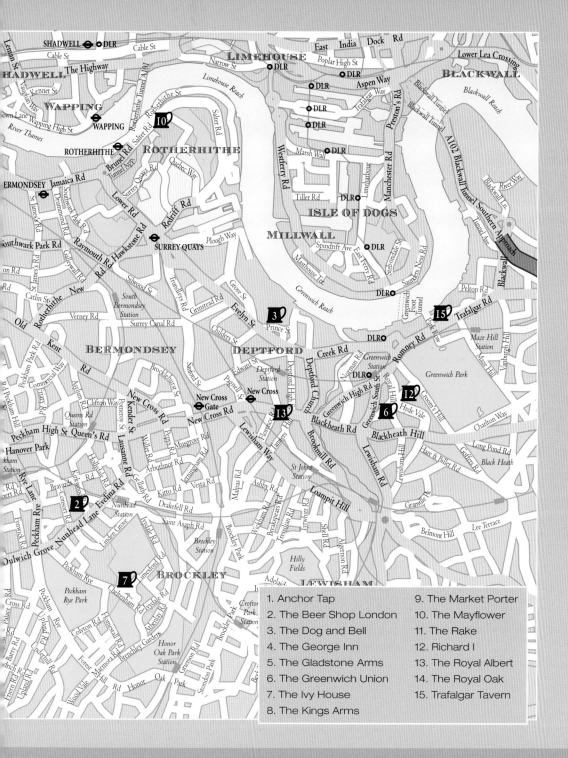

1. Anchor Tap
2. The Beer Shop London
3. The Dog and Bell
4. The George Inn
5. The Gladstone Arms
6. The Greenwich Union
7. The Ivy House
8. The Kings Arms
9. The Market Porter
10. The Mayflower
11. The Rake
12. Richard I
13. The Royal Albert
14. The Royal Oak
15. Trafalgar Tavern

Anchor Tap

20A Horsleydown Lane, Southwark SE1 2LN

BEERS: Sam Smith's Old Brewery Bitter, Taddy Lager, Cider Reserve, Wheat Beer, Double Four Lager, Alpine Lager

The Anchor Tap's unique atmosphere brings a touch of Yorkshire to the banks of the Thames

The Anchor Tap takes its name from the old Anchor Brewery, which, if you are standing on Tower Bridge facing south, is the joyously complicated building squeezed between the bridge and Butler's Wharf. The Anchor was one of many Southwark breweries that clustered along the Thames from the days of Queen Elizabeth I.

Today the Anchor Tap is owned by the Yorkshire brewery firm Sam Smith's of Tadcaster. The Yorkshiremen are to be greatly admired, for not only do they add an element of choice to London's beer market, but a careful pub-buying policy means that their London estate is of exceptionally high quality, and a large proportion of their pubs are celebrated in this book.

Although Sam Smith's owns fewer pubs than the two remaining London brewers, Young's and Fuller's, ounce for ounce the average Sam Smith's pub weighs several carats more than its rivals. As if this were not enough they also sell their beers considerably below normal London prices, despite having to ship it some 150 miles further than their London counterparts. This is due to the fact that Sam Smith's is one of those rare creatures – an unlimited company. There are only a handful of these, and shareholders have unlimited liability for company debts, but on the plus side the company's affairs are entirely transparent and the directors can do very much as they please without having markets or accountants tell them otherwise.

Sam Smith's unusual financial status has made a major contribution to the preservation of a significant number of important London buildings that would have been unlikely to fare so well under limited or public company ownership; the Anchor Tap is one of these. Frugal and uncluttered, the pub is reminiscent of the days when its customers were warehousemen, dockers and sailors. It actually has quite a northern feel to it, though this is by no means a feature of Sam Smith's London estate – quite the contrary. The Anchor Tap certainly benefits from being the best pub for quite a way in any direction, so bear this in mind when planning your day if you are thinking of visiting HMS Belfast, the Design Museum or any of Southwark's other attractions.

The Beer Shop London

40 Nunhead Green, London SE15 3QF

BEERS: Changing selection of local and interesting British beers direct from cask

London's first true micropub

The Rake (see p.210) is undoubtedly smaller than the Beer Shop London, but no one has ever thought of it as a micropub. The Beer Shop London, however, is definitely a micropub. What's the difference? It's like 'cool'. If you have to ask, you'll never know.

Owner and pretty much the only member of staff, Lee Gentry, discovered the phenomena that are the Broadstairs micropubs (the Chapel, the 39 Steps, the Four Candles) when visiting his mum, and liked the elegance of the idea that a simple focus on one element of the offering – in this case, beer – then allows the other aspects to just fall away. There are now more than 100 micropubs in the UK and they even have their own association, although Lee doesn't adhere to their slightly purist approach of being a place that 'shuns all forms of electronic entertainment and dabbles in traditional pub snacks'. No banning of mobile phones here.

Lee comes from a pub-running family and, after stints in a number of South London pubs including the Royal Albert (see pp.212–213), found a site that had once been a haberdashers and then a musical instrument repair shop before bringing a soupcon of glamour to unfashionable but upcoming Nunhead by reopening its doors as London's first micropub. (Some may object that Late Knights brewery in Penge got their first with the Beer Rebellion in Gipsy Hill, but it and its equally small and perfectly formed sisters are more tiny brewery taps than micropubs in the pure sense).

Lee is there pretty much all the time, so if his wife Lauren wants to see him, she must come down to the Beer Shop too. Happily she shares his vision as well as bringing him his supper, so you will see her behind the bar too at weekends. In order to get some time together, they don't open the pub on a Monday. This must cause a degree of consternation amongst their growing following of dedicated regulars, who for one night a week must entertain themselves, but there is no doubt that the pub enjoys considerable and passionate loyal support. As Lee put it, 'people tell us when they're going on holiday, so that we don't worry if we don't see them'. Isn't that a sign of a great pub?

THE DOG AND BELL

The Dog and Bell

116 Prince Street, Deptford SE8 3JD

BEERS: Fuller's London Pride, plus guests

This award-winning dockers' alehouse is particularly well thought of among beer aficionados and locals

Exclusivity always brings a certain extra enjoyment to any experience. It may come about as a result of selection (price, class, membership) or just happenstance. Frequently the best things in life are hard to find. George Orwell famously wrote about the perfect pub, which he called the Moon Under Water. The moon reflected in water is an intangible thing, and so, sadly, Orwell's pub never existed. Closer to hand, however, but definitely off the beaten track, is The Dog and Bell, and while no one would claim it is a perfect pub a visit is a considerably better use of time than a lifetime's search for the impossible.

A combination of those two magical ingredients, a real-ale pub and an honest-to-goodness locals' pub, The Dog and Bell is tucked away in a warren of Deptford's riverside streets, between the largely deserted former naval yard at Convoys Wharf and a recreation ground called, bizarrely, Twinkle Park. A regular entry in the Campaign For Real Ale's *Good Beer Guide* – the drinkers' bible – it has been lauded by the campaign as its southeast London pub of the year.

This one-bar pub displays its credentials in the shape of pump clips from well-drunk guest ales over the bar, and on its walls are a collection of rag-tag notices from locals which may range from a request for studio space from a pair of artists to the latest newspaper cutting charting the career of local-boy-made-good Jools Holland. Church-pew seating around the walls and high-backed chairs at the bar invite customers to sprawl. The energetically minded can play bar billiards, and outdoor types can take advantage of the walled beer garden. The River Thames is nearby, as is Deptford Market. Sunday night is the pub's quiz night.

The George Inn

77 Borough High Street, Southwark SE1 1NH

BEERS: George Ale, Greene King Abbot Ale, Fuller's London Pride, Flowers

Named after England's patron saint, this ancient galleried coaching inn is a true survivor and as such is one of England's national treasures

Without a shadow of doubt The George Inn is the most important pub in London, in that it is the last surviving Southwark galleried inn. There is much more history associated with The George than space here could even start to do justice to. So much so that its owners – the National Trust – have written a book laying out the story of The George, so the best advice is to go there and read it. Both William Shakespeare and Charles Dickens are known to have drunk here, and pretty much anyone who has been anyone has paid it a visit at one time or another.

Most famous of the Southwark inns was, of course, Geoffrey Chaucer's Tabard Inn, as depicted in his famous *The Canterbury Tales*, and the galleried portion of The George gives some idea of what The Tabard would have looked like. They were just two of many inns that crowded back to back – hence the galleries – along Borough High Street. Borough High Street was London's most important thoroughfare when London Bridge was the only connection between London (exclusively on the north of the river) and Southwark. Southwark was where Londoners played, as being outside the City it escaped many of the City's ordinances. Hence, all the theatres, the bull and bear rings and the brothels, or stews, were all located in Southwark.

The George's origins are obscure, but it was well established by the reign of Henry VIII (1509–47) and we know that one Nicholas Marten was landlord in 1558. In 1670 a fire which started in the rope store demolished part of the structure, and another fire in 1676 destroyed The George and another 500 Southwark dwellings. So, the oldest part of the inn is actually the ungalleried portion which was rebuillt after the fire, though the galleried part is also 17th-century and once extended to the two other sides of the courtyard.

The real business of inns like The George was waggoning – moving freight around the country in the days before rail. As centres of commerce the inns themselves became wealthy establishments, and as the nation's roads improved the significance of the trade improved too. The George added stage-coaching to the waggoning trade in the 18th century, but never became one of the top-quality coaching inns. Sadly the trade from both these businesses declined with the rise of the railways. This is why the lease on The George was only £6 per annum in 1828 but £150 per annum in 1668.

In the end, all the great Southwark inns fell victim to the railways, and Chaucer's Tabard Inn was demolished by property developers in 1875 despite a public outcry. Ironically, The George survived because it was bought by a railway, the Great Northern Railway Company, in 1873, who used the courtyard as a goods clearing yard for parcels and freight items moved by train. This function resulted in the destruction of the north and east galleries; the south side was saved only by the tenacity of the tenant.

The advent of the motorcar spelt the end of The George's function as an inn, but by this time its remarkable history and status were starting to be more widely appreciated, and in 1937 it was gifted to the National Trust, who took it over to ensure that we can continue to enjoy its many rooms and many pleasures today.

The Gladstone Arms

64 Lant St, Borough SE1 1QN

BEERS: Black Sheep Best Bitter

Cosy pub with an interesting history and one of the best (albeit tiny) spaces in which to experience a huge variety of music

Pub names offer historians a fascinating window onto London's social history, with names often reflecting local trades or popular figures of a certain time. This one was named after William Ewart Gladstone, the dominant personality in the Liberal Party from 1868–94, famed for his oratory and prime minister on four occasions; it is likely that the pub changed its name some time after his death. The current pub was built sometime in the 1920s, though a pub has stood on this site since 1840.

The Gladstone's customers are either locals who have lived in the area for many years or the new wave of arty types who have moved into this part of London. You do not have to be laid back to enjoy this pub, but it helps. It is both modern and traditional with a hint of the bohemian. Talking is certainly a feature at the Glad' today (W. E. G. would be proud). Open all day, several customers sit using the pub's free wi-fi on their laptops, others simply play chess or read a newspaper.

Charles Dickens once lived nearby and although there is no evidence that he drank at the Gladstone's predecessor (though he certainly drank in the nearby George Inn, which has a mention in Little Dorritt), just maybe he based the character of Bill Sikes on someone who drank here. Small though it may be, the Gladstone has a big heart. It is a survivor, coming through the Blitz of World War II and the post-war development that followed.

A moment's walk away from Borough underground station, the Gladstone has to be one of London's best music venues and a rare find in an area unrenowned for live bands. For long periods, the Gladstone has been closed and boarded up, but it is open once again and now hosts regular music nights – folk, blues, jazz, rock and acoustic all feature. There is no stage, hardly any room for a sound engineer let alone an audience, and certainly no changing room for the musicians, but it works. There is no charge for entry on music nights – normally Thursday, Friday and Saturday – if you want one of the few seats it is best to arrive early.

Draught Addlestones cloudy cider is served. The food, served at lunchtimes from Monday to Friday, consists of pies sourced from the justifiably famed Pieminister stall in nearby Borough Market (surely London's greatest foodie paradise).

The Greenwich Union

56 Royal Hill, Greenwich SE10 8RT

BEERS: Blonde Beer, House Ales

The Greenwich Union could be described as an alehouse of the future: it shuns national brewery products, preferring to champion high-quality lager and its own beer

Immediately next door to the traditional-looking Richard I (see p.211) is one of London's newest pubs. The Greenwich Union is named after a beer – Union – brewed by the Meantime Brewing Co. Ltd, which is also situated in Greenwich, and this is the first tied house of Britain's fastest-growing brewery firm. All the beers served come from the brewery, and the pub is unique in London for selling no national brewery products whatsoever, not even Guinness. The brewery is the brainchild of Brewmaster Alastair Hook, who trained at the world-famous brewing school at Weihenstephen near Munich in Bavaria (also home to the world's oldest brewery, dating back to 1044).

The Greenwich Union is an attempt at a fusion of the traditional pub and the contemporary bar, aiming to create the relaxed atmosphere of the pub with the emphasis on service and friendliness that many modern bars offer and which is increasingly central to the success of any commercial operation.

The result is that the Union has developed a keen following in a remarkably short period of time.

The long, thin pub opens out to a light, airy conservatory and a secluded beer garden. The pub has given a new young chef carte blanche to make his name, and sources ingredients for its dishes from the cheese shop, organic butcher and the fishmonger on this village street. The emphasis on local foods and local beers is one that consumers appreciate, and the Union uses the awareness of its customers to encourage them to think about beer in terms of food. This often leaves them pleasantly surprised.

If you ask for a taster set you will be given a sample of each of the beers to try before you settle on your favourite. In the chocolate stout, the raspberry beer and the wheat beer you will discover tastes and styles that will almost certainly be new to you. This is cutting-edge brewing and pub service, presented by people whose passion about the quality of their offering is infectious.

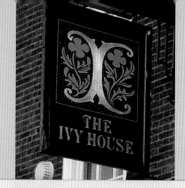

The Ivy House

40 Stuart Road, London SE15 3BE

BEERS: Changing range of largely very local ales and draught beers

A community-owned pub that works hard to entertain the community

Many London pubs are in this book because they are historic. The Ivy House is in because it makes history. Built in the 1930s by Truman's – undoubtedly the architecturally superior of all the big London brewers – it was constructed in the typical 'roadhouse' style encouraged by the Improved Public House movement of the inter-war years when a pub was allowed to look like anything at all, so long as it didn't look like a pub.

Originally called the Newlands Tavern, its long mock-Tudor interior makes it an ideal dance hall cum music event and this is what it was noted for many of the years of its life. The pub fell into decline, however, in the harsh economic climate of the 2000s and eventually closed in April 2012, at which point, like so many other pubs, it was scheduled for redevelopment into residential accommodation. That might have been the end of the story, were it not for the passage of the Localism Act 2011.

This created the legal concept of the Asset of Community Value. This is defined as 'land or property of importance to a local community' and therefore gains additional protection from development, as community organisations can nominate that something be registered as an asset of community value.

A dedicated group of locals took advantage of the act, banded together, created the Ivy House Community Pub Limited – a Community Benefit Society – and started to sell shares as a way of raising funds to buy the pub. They were successful, and, in their own words, 'the Ivy House is London's first co-operatively owned pub, the first pub in the UK to be listed as an Asset of Community Value, and the first building to be bought under the "community right to bid" provisions of the Localism Act.' It reopened in August 2013.

Today the company has 371 shareholders, who appoint a management team, which in turn appoints the pub's manager. The manager is kept pretty busy, not only looking after the fabric of this wood-panelled three-room pub, but also in booking a never-ending series of events. Not for the Ivy House the usual Tuesday pub quiz. Oh no! A regular newsletter informs locals of the long schedule of What's On coming their way; everything from French music evenings, poetry groups and knitting circles to lots and lots of live bands. It should not surprise you therefore to learn that the Ivy House won the English Heritage Angel Award for 'Best Rescue of A Historic Building 2013'.

The Kings Arms

25 Roupell Street, Southwark SE1 8TB

BEERS: Adnams Southwold, plus 8 rotating guest lines including a stout and at least two London breweries

This charming little two-bar pub was once a funeral directors, but all sombreness has long since been replaced by charm

A lovely little backstreet boozer in a terrace of immaculate Georgian two-up-two-downs, just to the rear of Waterloo East Station. The Kings Arms is a stylish operation and a wonderful example of the difference a little care and attention can make.

The pub is unusual in that it is one of the few to have resisted the temptation to knock the public and saloon bars together; they remain separated by a two-thirds-height wooden partition, adding to the cosy feeling on either side. The long public bar gets less natural light and consequently has a slightly darker feel, but it is tastefully decorated with a range of photographs of Roupell Street in years gone by. The saloon is more open, with a more eclectic range of decoration; the windows advertise the pub's continuous inclusion in the *Good Beer Guide*.

To the rear of the public bar is a dining room where Thai food is a speciality Monday through Saturday; a Sunday roast is served from 12.00pm-3.00pm on Sundays. The room is split between tables on the left and counter and stool seating along the walls; it is a pleasant and fun space under a conservatory roof and with a range of well-chosen clutter.

There is no shortage of things to see and do within a very easy walk of Roupell Street, and considering the paucity of decent pubs nearer the main tourist attractions, you would be well advised to make a beeline for The Kings Arms after a concert at the Royal Festival Hall or the Queen Elizabeth Hall. Similarly lacking a good pub closer at hand are the National Theatre, the National Film Theatre, the Museum of the Moving Image, the Hayward Gallery, the London Eye, the London Aquarium and the Imax cinema. In the other direction both the Young and the Old Vic are not too far.

The Market Porter

9 Stoney Street, Borough SE1 9AA

BEERS: Harvey's Sussex Bitter, plus 11 guests

It is very rare to catch this pub in a quiet moment, as it caters not only for Borough Market's traders and visitors but also for the numerous film crews who practically queue up to use characterful Park Street

There are several world-class 'ale' pubs in London: The White Horse in southwest London (see p.189), The Wenlock Arms in north London (see p.150) and the Market Porter in the southeast. Each is distinguished by an absolute belief in the qualities of a good pint of traditional English ale, and each ensures that its customers experience a constantly varying selection of the best of British.

The Market Porter is possibly the *primus inter pares* of this illustrious group in terms of the sheer range and variety of beers it offers. As the most centrally located and with a guaranteed seven-day-a-week trade, its ales turn over faster and therefore change faster too.

There has been a pub on the site since 1638, at which time it would have been one of scores of alehouses and inns clustered along Borough High Street in the days when London Bridge was the only crossing on the River Thames to the City of London. The Market Porter's proximity to Southwark Cathedral would also have brought it business, as would have the nearby Hop Exchange, where the hop crops from Kent, Sussex and Hampshire were traded and from which the many breweries gathered along the south bank of the Thames would have bought their supplies; there, too – thanks to the wild fluctuations in hop crop yields – fortunes were made and lost by speculators.

Today it is Borough Market that provides the lifeline, and as one of London's two remaining central markets (the other being Smithfield) Borough has ensured that the surrounding neighbourhood has remained largely unchanged. Any regular to the Market Porter will have seen film crews working in Park Street, which is still the most 'Dickensian-looking' street in London. The pub opens at 7.30am to cater for the market traders and closes again at 9am. Farmers' markets at the weekend keep the trade going, and even Sundays are busy with people travelling to the pub just to sample beers that they cannot get elsewhere.

The Mayflower

117 Rotherhithe Street, Rotherhithe SE16 4NF

BEERS: Six cask ales which change constantly, selected from various UK breweries

The Mayflower has been a veritable institution in Rotherhithe for four centuries thanks to its prime riverside location

This handsome old house was originally named either The Spread Eagle & Crown or The Shippe (authorities differ), but changed its name in 1957 – ensuring its survival – to The Mayflower, in memory of Captain Christopher Jones. Jones was a Rotherhithe man, who moored his ship The Mayflower nearby prior to its departure to collect religious refugees determined to make new lives in the New World in 1620. Rotherhithe was a likely place to find a ship prepared to make such a voyage, as both it and the neighbouring parish of Southwark were known as Dissenting strongholds in the early 17th century.

The pub itself dates from the 16th century, though the present structure is some 200 years younger. Sadly, the upper floor was blown off and destroyed in the Blitz, and the pub was further converted during the 1960s. Yet today it still has a 17th-century feel to it, and if you took the bar and all the trappings away it could resemble a Dissenters'

prayer hall. Settle seats are inscribed with words of wit and wisdom; walls are adorned with *Mayflower* memorabilia and prints of Rotherhithe from the days when it was a residential area supplying labour to the timber trade in Surrey Docks. Due to the fire risk the timber business was not welcome on the north side of the river and, accordingly, a whole quarter grew up around the trade. Until recently the pub doubled as a post office for the convenience of local sailors and, thanks to its American associations, it is still possible to buy American stamps here.

The Mayflower enjoys a riverside location, and a patio on piles driven into the riverbed extends out over the water. Captain Jones returned from his epic voyage in 1621, but tragically died shortly afterwards; he is buried in the neighbouring St Mary the Virgin Church. Next door to the pub is the engine room of the Rotherhithe Tunnel, which contains a working steam engine and exhibition.

The Rake

14a Winchester Walk, Borough Market SE1 9AG

BEERS: Large selection of global bottled beers, plus interesting draught and cask taps

A pioneering beer haven and possibly London's smallest pub

Since opening in August 2006 the Rake has rapidly become a much-loved London landmark. Its story is tied up with the now world-famous Borough Market, on the periphery of which it perches. It is very small.

Mike Hill and Richard Dinwoodie started Utobeer (a pun on Utopia) as Borough Market traders in 1998, having been impressed with the way Belgians presented beer. Having convinced the market trustees that they weren't planning a lager stall, they started selling the beers they liked, and found themselves riding the crest of the wave that was the food revolution that put Borough Market on the London map big time. The market stall developed into a wholesale business as they were approached by retailers and restaurateurs who wanted to put better beers in their bars, and then, as the business expanded, customers started asking where they could go to drink these beers. They realised that, with a few exceptions like the White Horse (see p.189), there wasn't anywhere, and so the idea of their own retail operation dawned on them.

The Rake was actually was a pub called the Kings Arms until 1944, when the surrounding tenements were torn down to allow for the expansion of the then-burgeoning wholesale fruit and veg market. The building survived as a market cafe rather than a pub. Being in the market Mike and Richard got wind that the cafe tenant was planning to leave and approached the market to let them have the retail space they wanted. At that point they were unaware of its previous pub life, and planned only a modest pop-up, but soon realised that as an ex-pub it had a proper cellar and their ambitions could expand. With the addition of proper draught lines it opened as allegedly London's smallest pub.

It majorly focuses on beer and sells no national brands, which had many people predicting its swift demise. A tiny wine and spirits offering is dwarfed by the beer range, and don't expect food. Privileged visitors are invited to sign the pub wall, which was inspired by the much-scribbled-on Hemingway Bar in Havana. Greg Keoch from Stone Brewing, San Diego was the first to leave a graffito. Since then hundreds of brewers from all over the world have followed suit. This author is one of them.

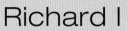

Richard I

52-54 Royal Hill, Greenwich SE10 8RT

BEERS: Young's Bitter, Young's Special, Young's Triple A

Lovingly known by most locals as the Tolly, this 18th-century pub is a rare east London outlet of southwest London brewers Young's

Ask a Greenwich resident to direct you to the best pub around and they will direct you to the Tolly, as the Richard I is affectionately known. Originally two 18th-century shops, one selling sweets and the other beer, the premises were acquired by the Tollemache and Cobbold Brewery of Ipswich and knocked together some time between 1920 and 1923. Young's Brewery added it to their portfolio as a far-flung outpost of their south-west London empire in 1974 during one of those periods of pub estate churning that goes on from time to time, but it is still known as the Tolly.

Royal Hill is the road up to the more genteel parts of Greenwich, and the pub certainly benefits from its seclusion. It is definitely the place to come for conversation or quiet contemplation of the newspaper without distraction or interruption. If you have not been before, choose the right-hand door into the main bar; the left-hand door is strictly for a select band of locals. If you can, grab the distinctive bay-window seat, which gives you a bird's-eye view of what is happening on Royal Hill. If it is sunny lose yourself in the large beer garden.

The Richard I is a great jumping-off point for Greenwich's many treasures. The 190-acre Greenwich Park, enclosed by the Duke of Gloucester between 1417 and 1437, is three minutes away. At the top of the hill in the park is the observatory, the foundation stone of which was laid in 1675. From here you can enjoy one of the best views of London; in the foreground is the Queen's House built for Anne of Denmark, wife of James I (1566–1625). The Queen's House stands in front of the former Royal Naval College built by Sir Christopher Wren, Nicholas Hawksmoor and Sir John Vanbrugh; the college stands on the site of the old Greenwich Palace, the favourite home of the Tudors and birthplace of Henry VIII in 1491, Mary I in 1516 and Elizabeth I in 1533.

The Royal Albert

460 New Cross Road, London SE14 6TJ

BEERS: Dark Star Hophead, Sharp's Doom Bar, plus changing guest ales and Volden house beer

An unfussy South London pub with a genuinely warm atmosphere

Deptford, with its naval yard associations, was once crowded with pubs. One list of extant and extinct establishments runs to 207 entries. The vast majority have disappeared, along with the navy. So the Royal Albert is something of a survivor.

It seems to have been somewhat unusual too in as much as since the days for which there are records of the pub – 1850 – it appears to have remained a free house throughout its history, never having fallen into the maws of one of the many London breweries it has so successfully outlasted.

For most of its life it has remained the Royal Albert; with the exception of one brief and unglamourous period as the blacked-out glass Paradise Bar which came to an end with the fatal shooting of a doorman. The pub always had a reputation for live music and the local band made good, Squeeze, played many of their early gigs there, as did a young lady by the name of Kate Bush.

Its unfortunate and seedy life as the Paradise Bar forced a brief closure on the premises, in which state it was found by the young pub group Antic, which specialises in lost causes and unusual premises, and which is noted for its idiosyncratic, slightly anarchic approach to décor, refurbishment and furnishings. In typical Antic fashion, when they found the old Royal Albert pub sign in the cellar, they just dusted it off and hung it back up again.

It opened as Antic's fifth or sixth pub in 2006 and hasn't changed much since. Despite initial appearances it's not actually a student pub – Goldsmith's College is nearby – as university academic and administrative staff are more likely to drop in than undergraduates themselves. Perhaps the atmosphere is just a bit too cosy and comfy for them.

Some rare and original features remain, notably in the form of windows and bar mirrors. There is a good range of interesting cask and craft ales on offer, complimented by simple fresh pub food, produced, as in all Antic pubs, by chefs who have autonomy over the menu. This is the kind of pub for a long evening with friends, just relaxing with a burger, a beer and a board game.

The Royal Oak

44 Tabard Street, Southwark SE1 4JU

BEERS: Harvey's Sussex Bitter, Harvey's Pale Ale, Harvey's Mild, Harvey's Armada

Beer is the main attraction here, though the Royal Oak is also notable for having retained its distinct public and saloon bars

As the sole London outlet of Sussex brewers Harvey's of Lewes, The Royal Oak is very much a magnet for beer lovers as well as representing a sympathetic rescue of a fine and unusual Victorian interior. Harvey's occupies an unusual place in the pantheon of UK brewers in that – along with Timothy Taylor's of Yorkshire – it is the most widely admired and respected within the brewing trade. When, in 1999, the River Ouse burst its banks and inundated the brewery, other rival brewers rallied round, offering casks, assistance with saving the yeast strain and – significantly – not poaching accounts when the brewery was down. As a result Harvey's, founded in 1790, was back in production in a remarkably short time, and its ardent band of followers could breathe a sigh of relief. The Jenner family who run the firm have had their share of adversity in recent years. The brewery was ravaged by fire only a few years before the flood. A plague of frogs is expected any time.

Harvey's Sussex Bitter is occasionally available in some of London's better beer establishments, but a pub offering the full range is a boon, and the chance of drinking them in such pleasant surroundings is an added bonus – the cast-iron pillars and ceiling plasterwork are original.

The entrance on Nebraska Street opens onto an office window in the bar, with a door to the saloon bar to the left and onto the public bar on the right, creating a separation of the kind that is now pretty rare. Pale eggshell walls in the public bar and richer burgundy colours in the saloon bar are judiciously hung with prints. In the public bar the prints are of a theatrical nature, reflecting the dramatic interests of brewery boss Miles Jenner. In the saloon the brewery itself is well represented.

Drinkers in the public bar have the odd sensation of looking at the back of the bar of the saloon as there is no corresponding frontage at head height. The sweeping lines created are very effective.

A little off the beaten track, perhaps, but the pub is still well situated to act as a staging post when exploring historic Southwark, and with Little Dorrit Street, Copperfield Street and Quilp Street all nearby the area's literary connections are not in doubt. Vinopolis, Southwark Cathedral and Tate Modern are all within walking distance. Looking west, the Imperial War Museum is a 10-minute walk.

Trafalgar Tavern

5 Park Row, Greenwich SE10 9NG

BEERS: Fuller's London Pride, Flowers Bitter, plus guests

Fans of Charles Dickens should recognize the Trafalgar Tavern from the wedding feast described in Our Mutual Friend

It is hard to contemplate, but only a little over 200 years ago Greenwich was a fishing village, and, in season, one of the catches yielded up by the River Thames was whitebait. Nowadays the River Thames is not quite so prolific, but the Trafalgar Tavern is still *the* place in London to go and eat a whitebait dinner. In the 19th century senior Liberals and Tories would annually board rival barges and sail down the Thames for such a dinner.

At the Trafalgar these dinners would have taken place in what is now the Lord Nelson Room, which offers a view of the broad sweep of the Thames as it embraces the Isle of Dogs. To the powerful leaders of the world's largest empire – from whose far-flung corners raw materials of all sorts came and to where the finished goods were sent – the numbers of ships passing beneath the Trafalgar's bay windows must have been a truly gratifying sight. The view fom the Trafalgar today is still impressive, albeit quite different.

The Trafalgar was built in 1837 by Joseph Kay, a founder member of the Royal Institute of British Architects and surveyor of Greenwich Hospital, on the site of a tavern called The George. It ceased being a pub in 1915, when it became a club named the Royal Alfred Aged Merchant Seamen's Institute. Fortunately, in 1965 it reverted to being the Trafalgar once more. Given that even today great and historic pubs and their interiors are not being retained, the Trafalgar's story must count as one of the most remarkable restorations in London's history.

PUB ADDRESSES, WEBSITES & TRANSPORT LINKS

The West End

The Argyll Arms
18 Argyll Street W1F 7TP
TUBE: Oxford Circus

The Blue Posts
28 Rupert Street W1D 6DJ
TUBE: Leicester Square

The Champion
13 Wells Street W1T 3PA
TUBE: Tottenham Court Road

Cittie of Yorke
22 High Holborn WC1V 6BS
TUBE: Holborn

The Coal Hole
91 Strand WC2R
TUBE: Charing Cross

The Cock
27 Great Portland Street
  W1W 8QG
TUBE: Oxford Circus

The Cross Keys
31 Endell Street WC2H 9BA
TUBE: Covent Garden,Holborn

The Dog & Duck
18 Bateman Street W1D 3AJ
TUBE: Tottenham Court Road

The Dover Castle
43 Weymouth Mews W1G 7EH
TUBE: Regent's Park

Euston Tap
190 Euston Road NW1 2EF
www.eustontap.com
TUBE: Euston

The Fitzroy Tavern
16 Charlotte Street W1T 2LY
TUBE: Goodge Street

The French House
49 Dean Street W1 5BG
www.frenchhousesoho.com
TUBE: Tottenham Court Road

The Guinea
30 Bruton Place W1J 6NL
www.theguinea.co.uk
TUBE: Bond Street, Green Park

The Harp
47 Chandos Place WC2N 4HS
TUBE: Charing Cross

The Lamb
92 Lamb's Conduit Street
  WC1N 3LZ
TUBE: Holborn

Lamb & Flag
33 Rose Street WC2E 9EB
TUBE: Covent Garden

The Nell Gwynne
1–2 Bull Inn Court, London
  WC2R 0NP
TUBE: Charing Cross, Leicester
  Square, Covent Garden

The Porterhouse
21–22 Maiden Lane WC2E 7NA
www.porterhousebrewco.com
TUBE: Charing Cross

Princess Louise
208 High Holborn WC1V 7BW
TUBE: Holborn

The Queens Larder
1 Queen Square WC1 3AR
www.queenslarder.co.uk
TUBE: Russell Square

The Red Lion
Crown Passage SW1Y 6PP
TUBE: Green Park

The Red Lion
2 Duke of York Street SW1Y 6JP
TUBE: Green Park, Piccadilly Circus

The Red Lion
48 Parliament Street SW1A 2NH
TUBE: Westminster

The Salisbury
90 St Martin's Lane WC2N 4AP
TUBE: Leicester Square

The Seven Stars
53 Carey Street WC2A 2JB
TUBE: Holborn, Temple

The Ship & Shovell
1–3 Craven Passage WC2N 5PH
TUBE: Embankment

Star & Garter
62 Poland Street W1F 7NX
TUBE: Oxford Circus

City & East End

The Black Friar
174 Queen Victoria Street
  EC4V 4EG
TUBE: Blackfriars

The Black Lion
Plaistow High Street E13 0AD
www.blacklionplaistow.co.uk
TUBE: Plaistow

The Cockpit
7 St Andrew's Hill EC4V 5BY
TUBE: Blackfriars

Dickens Inn
St Katharine's Dock E1W 1UH
www.dickensinn.co.uk
TUBE: Tower Hill

Fox & Anchor
115 Charterhouse Street
  EC1M 6AA
www.foxandanchor.com
TUBE: Farringdon

The Grapes
76 Narrow Street E14 8BP
TUBE: Limehouse (DLR)

The Hand & Shears
1 Middle Street EC1A 7JA
TUBE: Barbican

Hoop & Grapes
47 Aldgate High Street EC3N 1AL
TUBE: Aldgate

The Jerusalem Tavern
55 Britton Street EC1M 5UQ
www.stpetersbrewery.co.uk
TUBE: Farringdon

Lamb Tavern
Leadenhall Market EC3V 1LR
www.lambtavernleadenhall.com
TUBE: Aldgate

The Old Bell
95 Fleet Street EC4Y 1DH
TUBE: Blackfriars, Temple

Old Red Lion
418 St John Street EC1V 4NJ
www.oldredliontheatre.co.uk
TUBE: Angel

The Palm Tree
127 Grove Rd, London E3 5RP
TUBE: Mile End

The Pride of Spitalfields
3 Heneage Street E1 5LJ
TUBE: Aldgate East

The Punch Tavern
99 Fleet Street EC4Y 1DE
www.punchtavern.com
TUBE: Blackfriars, Temple

The Royal Oak
73 Columbia Road E2 7RG
www.royaloaklondon.com
TUBE: Liverpool Street

The Three Kings
7 Clerkenwell Close EC1R 0DY
TUBE: Farringdon

The Viaduct Tavern
126 Newgate Street EC1A 7AA
TUBE: St Paul's

Ye Old Cheshire Cheese
145 Fleet Street EC4A 2BU
TUBE: Blackfriars, Temple

Ye Old Mitre Tavern
Ely Place EC1N 6SJ
TUBE: Chancery Lane

Marylebone to Belgravia

Anglesea Arms
15 Selwood Terrace SW7 3QG
www.capitalpubcompany.com/
  anglesea
TUBE: South Kensington

The Antelope
22 Eaton Terrace SW1W 8EZ
TUBE: Sloane Square

The Grenadier
Old Barrack Yard, Wilton Row
  SW1X 7NR
TUBE: Hyde Park Corner

The Iron Duke
11 Avery Row W1K 4AN
TUBE: Bond Street

Nag's Head
53 Kinnerton Street, SW1 8ED
TUBE: Knightsbridge

The Queen's Arms
30 Queen's Gate Mews SW7 5QL
www.thequeensarmskensington.
  co.uk
TUBE: Gloucester Road

Queen's Head & Artichoke
30–32 Albany Street NW1 4EA
www.theartichoke.net
TUBE: Great Portland Street

The Star Tavern
6 Belgrave Mews West SW1X 8HT
TUBE: Knightsbridge

The Victoria
10a Strathearn Place W2 2NH
TUBE: Lancaster Gate

The Warrington
93 Warrington Crescent W9 1EH
www.gordonramsey.com/
  thewarrington
TUBE: Warwick Avenue

The Windsor Castle
27–29 Crawford Place W1H 4LJ
TUBE: Edgware Road

North London

The Albert
11 Princess Road NW1 8JR
TUBE: Chalk Farm

The Albion
10 Thornhill Road N1 1HW
www.the-albion.co.uk
TUBE: Highbury & Islington, Angel

The Assembly House
292–4 Kentish Town Road
  NW5 2TG
TUBE: Kentish Town

The Bohemia
762–764 High Road, London
  N12 9QH
www.thebohemia.co.uk
TUBE: Woodside Park

**Brewhouse and Kitchen
(Islington)**
5 Torrens Street, London
  EC1V 1NQ
www.brewhouseandkitchen.com/
  islington
TUBE: Angel

Camden Head
Camden Passage N1 8DY
TUBE: Angel

The Craft Beer Co. (Islington)
55 White Lion Street, London,
  N1 9PP
www.thecraftbeerco.com/pubs/
  islington
TUBE: Angel

The Flask
14 Flask Walk NW3 1HE
TUBE: Hampstead

Holly Bush
22 Holly Mount NW3 6SG
TUBE: Hampstead

The Jolly Butchers
4 Stoke Newington High Street
  N16 7HU
www.jollybutchers.co.uk
TRAIN: Stoke Newington (BR)

The Junction Tavern
101 Fortess Road NW5 1AG
www.junctiontavern.co.uk
TUBE: Kentish Town, Tufnell Park

King's Head
115 Upper Street N1 1QN
www.kingsheadtheatre.org
TUBE: Highbury & Islington, Angel

The Pineapple
51 Leverton Street NW5 2NX
TUBE: Kentish Town

Princess of Wales
22 Chalcott Road NW1 8LL
TUBE: Chalk Farm

Quinn's
65 Kentish Town Road NW1 8NY
TUBE: Camden Town

Southampton Arms
139 Highgate Road NW5 2RF
www.thesouthamptonarms.co.uk
TUBE: Tufnell Park

Spaniards Inn
Spaniards Road NW3 7JJ
www.thespaniardshampstead.
  co.uk
TUBE: Hampstead

The Washington
50 Englands Lane NW3 4UE
www.thewashingtonhampstead.
  co.uk
TUBE: Belsize Park, Chalk Farm

The Wenlock Arms
26 Wenlock Road N1 7TA
www.wenlock-arms.co.uk
TUBE: Old Street

The Widow's Son
75 Devons Rd, London E3 3PJ
TUBE: Devons Road (DLR)

West London

Blue Anchor
13 Lower Mall W6 9DJ
TUBE: Hammersmith

Britannia
1 Allen Street W8 6UX
www.britanniakensington.co.uk
TUBE: High Street Kensington

The Bulls Head
15 Strand on the Green W4 3PQ
TRAIN: Kew Bridge (BR)

The Churchill Arms
119 Kensington Church Street
   W8 7LN
TUBE: High Street Kensington

The Colton Arms
187 Greyhound Rd, London
   W14 9SD
TUBE: Barons Court, West
   Kensington

The Cow
89 Westbourne Park Road
   W2 5QH
www.thecowlondon.co.uk
TUBE: Westbourne Park

The Dove
19 Upper Mall W6 9TA
TUBE: Ravenscourt Park

The Fox & Pheasant
1 Billing Road SW10 9UJ
TUBE: Fulham Broadway

The Prince Edward
73 Princes Square W2 4NY
TUBE: Bayswater

The Tabard
Bath Road W4 1LW
TUBE: Turnham Green

Windsor Castle
114 Campden Hill Road W8 7AR
www.thewindsorcastlekensington
   .co.uk
TUBE: Notting Hill Gate

Southwest London

The Alma
499 Old York Road SW18 1TF
   www.almawandsworth.com
TRAIN: Wandsworth Town (BR)

The Antelope
76 Mitcham Rd, London
   SW17 9NG
www.theantelopepub.com
TUBE: Tooting Broadway

Balham Bowls Club
7-9 Ramsden Rd, London
   SW12 8QX
www.balhambowlsclub.com
TRAIN: Balham (BR)

The Devonshire
39 Balham High Road SW12 9AN
www.thedevonshirebalham.co.uk
TUBE: Balham

Duke of Cambridge
228 Battersea Bridge Road
   SW11 3AA
www.thedukeofcambridge.com
TRAIN: Clapham Junction (BR)

Duke's Head
8 Lower Richmond Road
   SW15 1JN
www.dukesheadputney.co.uk
TUBE: Putney Bridge

The Nightingale
97 Nightingale Lane SW12 8NX
TRAIN: Wandsworth Common (BR)

The Ship
41 Jews Row SW18 1TB
www.theship.co.uk
TRAIN: Wandsworth Town (BR)

Spread Eagle
71 Wandsworth High Street
  SW18 2PT
TRAIN: Wandsworth Town (BR)

The White Horse
Parson's Green Lane SW6 4UL
www.whitehorsesw6.com
TUBE: Parson's Green

The Woodman
60 Battersea High Street
SW11 3HX
TRAIN: Clapham Junction (BR)

Ye White Hart
The Terrace, Riverside SW13 0NR
TRAIN: Barnes Bridge (BR)

Southeast London

Anchor Tap
20A Horsleydown Lane SE1 2LN
TUBE: London Bridge, Tower Hill

The Beer Shop London
40 Nunhead Green, London
  SE15 3QF
www.thebeershoplondon.co.uk
TRAIN: Nunhead (BR)

The Dog and Bell
116 Prince Street SE8 3JD
TRAIN: Deptford (BR)

The George Inn
77 Borough High Street SE1 1NH
TUBE: London Bridge

The Gladstone Arms 64
Lant St SE1 1QN
TUBE: Borough

The Greenwich Union
50 Royal Hill SE10 8RT
www.greenwichunion.com
TUBE: Greenwich (DLR)

The Ivy House
40 Stuart Rd, London SE15 3BE
www.ivyhousenunhead.com
TRAIN: Nunhead, Honor Oak Park
  (BR)

The Kings Arms
25 Roupell Street SE1 8TB
TUBE: Southwark

The Market Porter
9 Stoney Street SE1 9AA
TUBE: London Bridge

The Mayflower
117 Rotherhithe Street SE16 4NF
TUBE: Rotherhithe (DLR)

The Rake
14a Winchester Walk, Borough
   Market SE1 9AG
www.utobeer.co.uk/the-rake
TUBE: London Bridge

Richard I
52–54 Royal Hill SE10 8RT
www.richardthefirst.co.uk
TUBE: Greenwich (DLR)

The Royal Albert
460 New Cross Rd, London
   SE14 6TJ
www.royalalbertpub.com
TRAIN: New Cross (BR)

The Royal Oak
44 Tabard Street SE1 4JU
TUBE: Borough

Trafalgar Tavern
5 Park Row SE10 9NW
www.trafalgartavern.co.uk
TUBE: Cutty Sark (DLR)
TRAIN: Maize Hill (BR)

Websites

www.camra.org.uk
An independent organization
   that promotes real ale.

www.beerintheevening.com
Features recommendations for
   over 40,000 pubs, bars and
   clubs in the UK.

www.fancyapint.com
News, features and reviews on
   a selection of British pubs.

www.belgianbeerguide.co.uk
Pubs and bars serving
   Belgian beer.

www.pubs.com
Features on London's best pubs
   and a handy pub finder.

www.meantimebrewing.com
Full lowdown on the Meantime
   Brewing Company, including
   beer stockists and pub.